D 101

Ideas for clubs and societies

Ideas for clubs and societies

Christine Fagg

An imaginative guide to planning
programmes and activities

Elek Books Limited
2 All Saints Street London N 1

Also by Christine Fagg

Raise cash – have fun

Imaginative ideas for fêtes, bazaars,
social functions and all kinds of
money-making entertainment

Be my guest

A guide to imaginative entertaining

Life and Leisure

Published by
ELEK BOOKS LIMITED
2 All Saints Street London N1

ISBN 0.236.15403.6

Made and printed in Great Britain by
Weatherby Woolnough Ltd., Wellingborough, Northants.

Contents

The mime
A pageant
Music and song
Dancing
Film shows
Mannequin parades
Pantomimes
The variety show
Copyright

Acknowledgements

I would like to thank the staff of Hitchin Library and the innumerable societies, organizations and individuals who have helped me personally in the production of this book. Included among these are:

The Association of '62 Clubs

Lions International

Members of the Association of Inner Wheel Clubs in Great Britain and Ireland

Members of the National Association of Ladies Circles

The National Association of Round Tables of Great Britain and Ireland

The National Association of Women's Clubs

The National Federation of Women's Institutes

The National Housewives Register

The National Union of Townswomen's Guilds

Rotary International

Introduction

Up and down the country—in towns, villages, city housing developments, rural council estates and suburbia, people join clubs or if they're enterprising, get together to form their own. Why? There are many different reasons. They may want to enjoy themselves and make friends, learn a subject, develop creative talent, partake in sports, improve community facilities or promote their political party, but they all have one thing in common: a desire to join with others for the mutual benefit and promotion of a shared interest.

As a journalist I have frequently been involved in answering letters from readers and two questions which regularly come up from club organizers are: 'We're running out of ideas for next year's programme—can you help?' Or, 'The members of our society have suddenly started to drift away—where have we gone wrong?' This book is written mainly to answer those questions. I have suggested numbers of ways in which organizers can plan exciting programmes, avoid the common pitfalls, keep members happy and attract new ones. There is also a chapter giving detailed information for those who would like to start up their own society.

Because my own personal experience has been to a great extent connected with women's clubs, it is inevitable that many of the ideas have been culled from this source. Nevertheless, I hope that the suggestions will help societies of all kinds whether for men, women, teenagers or clubs of mixed membership. The purpose of the clubs may be diverse, from purely social to such specific objectives as model engineering, natural history, home safety, studying beetles or collecting beermats. Such clubs may not require advice on talks, demonstrations, debates or discussions, but almost every society needs to organize, publicize, fund raise and to run the occasional social event as well as possibly mount an exhibition.

All societies are formed to meet a specific need and nothing should be allowed to eclipse this important factor. For instance, floral art enthusiasts want demonstrations from experts, not coffee mornings, socials and outings, unless of course it is to flower shows or exhibitions. Similarly, young wives may club together for friendship and inspiration for body, mind and spirit, but if say, the leadership concentrates on drama, although it may attract some, it will lose the majority of others. Therefore organizers should always bear the aims and objects of their society firmly in mind when planning their programmes.

Why is it that some clubs are a success right from the start and others go through bad patches which get longer and longer and sometimes result in the whole thing petering out? Let us first consider what it is a club of ANY type should provide. Of course, all will supply the material things like a place to meet, chairs to sit on and a cup of tea or coffee, but remember the following reasons for which it basically exists.

1 **An aim and an object** The success of a club lies above all in the amount of effort and drive it generates in order to achieve its aim and object. Everything should stem from this force, the content of the programmes and the activities both within the society and outside it. If it is a photographic club then speakers, outings and entertainments will all be concerned with that subject. If it is a chess club, a poultry-keeping association, a club for bell ringers or supporters of the football team, the same principles apply and much of the information in this book can be adapted to suit any society's personal requirements.

2 **Friendship** This is probably the most important benefit which membership of a club brings, and sharing your interest, be it rambling, under-water swimming, reading poetry or whatever, will help to overcome loneliness which is one of the greatest problems of our time. People may have different backgrounds, careers, religions, outlooks and problems, but from this variety of human personalities we are drawn into new friendships which will enhance and enrich the future.

3 **Education** Belonging to a club brings with it the opportunity to become better informed and to explore interests of all kinds. Whether you belong to the chrysanthemum club or a society to explore psychical research, contact with fellow members will bring knowledge of all kinds of specialized subjects and will stimulate the mind and open up fresh fields of study and enlightenment. Bursaries and grants are supplied by some existing organizations to help members to further their education in special courses held all over the country and occasionally abroad.

4 **Contribution to the Community** Many clubs, especially religious organizations, contribute in a practical way by looking outwards for ways in which to improve their community. In recent years this activity has become widespread and all kinds of clubs often apportion some of their time and funds for this purpose. This service may take the form of helping the needy in their homes or raising money to help worthy local causes. Parent-teacher organizations may campaign to install a Belisha beacon, and women's organizations a bus to take shoppers to town on market day. Many improvements within a community can be brought about more easily and with greater speed when members of a club voice one opinion.

What other ingredients are required to keep members happy and attract new ones? Having talked to many organizers of recreational, cultural, professional, political and special interest clubs all over Britain, various facts emerge. Naturally there is no simple solution but here, gathered from a number of experienced organizers, are some of the more common pitfalls into which a club may fall.

Proper organization of the club is essential if it is to run smoothly, have a happy atmosphere and be successful. This means team work amongst the committee members and attention to detail as well as adequate communication between them and the members. It's no good expecting people to take an interest in, or back up schemes about which they have heard nothing. Important announcements should be made twice because members often miss hearing them the first time.

Advance planning is very important indeed. A hand-to-mouth existence, when no definite arrangements are made until the last minute will lead to continual half-heartedness and loss of members. Everybody likes to feel secure in whatever they do and a solid framework of dates on a printed programme at the beginning of the club year means that members can plan their own lives around it to a great extent.

The chairman and secretary should get into the habit of carrying a flat, spiral notebook and writing everything down in it such as announcements, things to be done, speakers and their subjects, numbers present and so on. This ensures that all vital information is easily passed over to someone else in case of an emergency. All programme material, too, should be filed and kept together as well as ideas for future programmes. An emergency programme (see page 30) is a wise precaution in case a speaker fails to turn up.

Committee members should arrive well in advance of the starting time. If members arrive and find nothing 'on the go' it is a sure way to lose them. And see there is a notice at the entrance to the building clearly directing possible new members to the room in which the meeting is being held.

In order that there should be smooth continuity in the running of a club, make sure key personnel have deputies to learn the job during their last year of office. The chaos of losing all the members of a committee at the same time is avoided if one third stand down at the end of each year.

It is wise to have a rule that each committee member stands down for one year before re-election. This is the most tactful way to break up dominating 'factions' which are likely to develop in any society. It is a common and unfortunate fact that many people join a club and rise from the ranks to the committee in order to satisfy their own personal motives. Often they make excellent leaders, but at the same time it is necessary and essential for the good of all concerned that they are replaced by new blood.

The key to a happy and effective club rests to a very large extent upon the interest and care shown to each member by the chairman and secretary. If members don't turn up to meetings they should find out what has happened. Perhaps they are ill or in trouble or may just need a friend to call for them, but this thoughtful gesture will be greatly appreciated.

The chairman and secretary should also make a real effort to memorize every name so that they are in a position to greet members individually and to introduce one to another. This personal touch banishes that forlorn feeling from which almost everybody suffers when entering a roomful of unknown people. A warm welcome strikes a chord which in turn cannot fail to bring forth a response. If members are willing to give something to a club rather than just take from it, the chances of its success are considerably increased. But don't expect volunteers to offer to help a special project without encouragement. Go round and ask people individually, dividing the task up amongst the committee so that each one approaches a given number of members.

Speaking personally, I have had so much fun in belonging to a great variety of clubs and societies that it would be difficult to single out which one has given me most pleasure. Probably it was my first, when a gang of us from early schooldays started the 'Nacton Nippers' Club'. We had to ride up and down the garden path without holding on to the handlebars of our bicycles, climb a rope ladder to the top of the oak tree and fly a kite which we'd made ourselves in order to become members at all! Later we turned our attention to more worthy pastimes and all these experiences taught me a lot about what makes a club work.

The essence of a club should be in its adaptability and movement. It also depends a great deal upon each person giving something to keep it thriving and it is up to organizers to find out and make use of each member's ability and exploit it. A club prospers when every individual in it feels he or she is contributing in some small but vital way to its success. For this reason I hope the book will be read not only by presidents, chairmen, secretaries and committee members, but by all those people who form the body of any society.

Sometimes I go into a remote village hall where members have joined together for their weekly or monthly meeting. The building may have seen better days, the piano may be out of tune and the furniture well and truly worn. But through it all shines the warmth of companionship, the knowledge that pleasure is derived from sharing common interests and a powerful feeling comes over me that surely, this is what life is all about.

Gone is the old image of joining a club to pass the time. Now members are adventurous, open-minded and aware of the wider fields to explore. This book sets out to show how to make your club more go-ahead and enterprising, more purposeful and worthwhile and at the same time bring more fun, pleasure and enjoyment into the lives of all those who belong to it.

Chapter 1

Talks and demonstrations

The club programme is the life blood of any society and the success of each meeting depends a great deal upon the quality of the speaker. If the subject is attractive to the members it will draw them to the meeting like a magnet and next time they'll bring along their friends. Many a club membership has increased because of a run of stimulating speakers and demonstrators.

The view is often put forward nowadays that television, with its talks, documentaries and other informative programmes, brings the world to us. Why then, do we need to go out to listen to an artist talk about his passion for painting, a mountaineer describe his gruelling climb to the summit of a peak, or to see an expert on millinery create a hat?

The answer lies in the mystery of the human personality and because the personal contact between a speaker and his audience is real and tangible. No film, television programme or sound track is ever going to replace this factor. It explains why a wizened eighty-year-old gentleman who, years ago, spoke to our women's society about his lifetime spent in producing tapestries for churches has never been forgotten. And why only the other day, at a parent-teacher meeting, a faith healer held us spellbound for three hours giving a vivid account of her successes and failures. It is this direct communication with others which adds sparkle to our lives and inspiration to the daily round.

How, you may wonder, can good speakers be captured to inspire the members of your society? Your meetings may take place in the sparsely populated Yorkshire Moors, in a remote village in the Black Mountains or in a small farming community in East Anglia. It is often difficult to persuade speakers to travel long distances and the nearest town may be some miles away. Perhaps the varied interests and backgrounds of your members present difficulties and their ages may range from eighteen to ninety. There are special problems too, when new housing estates are grafted on to villages which have been in existence for centuries. Brand new married couples, some straight from the hectic life of large towns, others from a stimulating university or college training course, are all plunged together into the very different atmosphere of rural life. What a challenge for club organizers to provide entertaining speakers to satisfy everybody!

Certainly it would be impossible for me or anybody else to provide all the answers, but you cannot please all people all the time. And can you not recall a meeting in the past where there was to be a talk on a subject which you imagined held no interest for you? Once a speaker from The Royal Society for the Protection of Birds described the plight of the seagulls stranded on oil soaked beaches. As a result a friend of mine now regularly works part-time in a voluntary capacity for this society. A business man I know changed his job to a lesser paid, but more rewarding career in the service of Dr Barnardo after hearing a moving account from somebody working in this field. Such incidents are commonplace and many unlikely subjects lead members on to new outlets, hobbies, interests and careers. Do not therefore dismiss the opportunity to present the unusual, the daring and original, as well as the more popular run-of-the-mill subjects.

Advance planning

Before putting forth concrete suggestions for talks and demonstrations, a word about the advance planning of programmes. Organizers would be well advised to book speakers as far ahead as is reasonably possible, either on a three monthly or seasonal basis, or better still, a year ahead. This way there is more chance of getting the best material and it also makes for a well-oiled, smooth-running society.

Inviting speakers

When writing to invite speakers to your club, certain vital information should be included. But above all, do make it clear if the meeting is to take any special form. To illustrate this point clearly, readers might like to hear what happened to me last year.

I was invited by a group of young wives to speak at their special anniversary meeting. The letter stated that the evening would begin with a service in the church followed by a supper and then party games. Having just written a book on entertaining which had been published the previous month, I naturally assumed that this was the reason for the invitation and accordingly prepared a frivolous talk.

On arrival at the meeting, I enquired whether I was to speak before or after supper. Imagine my horror on being told 'Oh now! We want you to give the address in the service.' I leave it to the imagination of readers to register how I felt when mounting the steps to the pulpit! My light-hearted talk on entertaining had to be discarded completely and exchanged rapidly for something much more sober and appropriate.

Other information to include when inviting speakers is as follows:—

1   Give the recipient an idea of the character of your society. How many members belong? What is their average age? Is any interest shared by them all?
2   Offer a choice of dates if possible.
3   State the time the talk is to start and finish and the time allowed for questions.
4   Suggest the subject you would most like the speaker to talk about.

5　Ask for a statement of fees and expenses.
6　Enquire whether he needs any special equipment, hospitality or meals.

Sample letters
Here I have given a sample letter which applies to a Natural History Society.

R. E. Pullen, Esq.,
42 Mattock Drive,
North Fordingham,
Northamptonshire.　　　　　　　　　　　　　　14th October 197—

Dear Mr Pullen,
　We, the Southbridge Natural History Society, are compiling our programme for next year. Would you consider coming along to one of our meetings to give a talk on the Bedstraw Hawkmoth?
　We have a membership of forty-five men and women whose ages range from eighteen to eighty. Some are serious university students and teachers, others are merely interested in the subject as a hobby, but all are keen members who would like to know more about the Bedstraw Hawkmoth.
　We meet on the last Thursday in the month at Southbridge Town Hall at 7.30 p.m. and your talk would begin at 8 p.m. We allow three quarters of an hour for the talk and ten minutes or so for questions afterwards. At the moment we have the following dates free in 197—: 24th February, 27th April, and 30th November.
　We would appreciate an early reply to this request and if you are able to accept one of these dates, would you let us know your fee and expenses and also the title of your talk with a few details about yourself and activities.
　We do hope one of these dates will be convenient.
　　　　　　　　　　　　　　Yours sincerely,
　　　　　　　　　　　　　　　　Arthur Smith

Enclose a stamped addressed envelope for a reply and if this is in the affirmative, write again confirming the booking.

Dear Mr Pullen,

We are delighted to hear that you are able to speak to the Southbridge Natural History Society at Southbridge Town Hall on 24th February 197— at 8 p.m. We note the title of your talk will be The Life of the Bedstraw Hawkmoth and the Carabid Beetle. We are agreeable to your fee of £2.50 plus travelling expenses of 4p per mile.

I enclose a map which I hope will make it a simple matter to find Southbridge Town Hall. There is ample car parking space beside it.

If you require any special equipment perhaps you would let me know and I will do my best to supply your needs.

We all look forward to meeting you on 24th February next year.

Yours sincerely,

Arthur Smith.

Two weeks before the meeting takes place, telephone the speaker, or send him a short note, reminding him once again of the arrangement and include travelling instructions.

Note the mention of the enclosed map giving directions to the Town Hall. It is a simple task to duplicate a hand-drawn map clearly marking the hall where your meetings take place. On one occasion, a weary speaker floundered up and down through a maze of muddy lanes on a wet winter night. 'Turn left by a ruined church on the right', wrote a bright secretary in her letter dated 17th June. But on the dark November night of the meeting, the church, hidden among trees behind a high wall, was completely obscured. Result? An enraged speaker, who arrived half an hour late, unable to give of his best to an audience who appeared oblivious to his difficulties.

It is a good idea for secretaries to find out where their electric plug fitments are placed in the hall and whether they are 5 amp. (two or three pin), 15 amp. (three pin) or 13 amp. (flat pin) type, so that they can give an intelligent answer to questions about lighting from a speaker who may want to bring electrical equipment such as a slide projector.

Finding local speakers

Let us now assume that the following year stretches ahead and that against the date of each meeting there is a blank space. How will you set about finding speakers? If you are a fairly new society, small in number and running on a tight budget, economy is an obvious essential. Turn first to local sources where you should find some informative speakers who often make no charge or ask only a nominal fee. Apart from this obvious advantage, there is nothing more satisfactory than a well recommended speaker who lives in the district. He or she is not likely to let you down because of bad weather, traffic jams or national disasters.

Consider first the Local Authority (see classified telephone directory) whose officers are sometimes prepared to describe the work of their departments and the effect upon the residents and what is provided by the rates we pay. Under this heading comes the curator of the museum, the librarian, the fire prevention officer, the surveyor, the registrar of births and deaths, the director of the public cleansing department, the parks director (who may also deal with the care of pot plants and indoor gardening) and the chairman and members of the local council.

The Local Education Authority offers a wealth of possibilities. Teachers from all types of school, from nursery to adult education, can be approached to give talks on their subjects. These range from domestic sciences and art in all its forms, to history, biology and technological subjects. Contact the Youth Employment Officer for talks on careers.

The Health and Welfare Departments with their highly trained staff of health visitors, midwives, child care officers, child psychologists, probation officers and other workers are all people with wide and interesting experiences of the problems of others. Into this category come hospital matrons, administrators and many other employees such as family planning experts, marriage guidance counsellors, medical social workers and magistrates.

Don't dismiss the idea of talks on religion which can be helpful concerning personal problems. Some organizations place a taboo upon this subject, but others like to learn about the faith of the Latter Day Saints, the Seventh Day Adventists, the Spiritualists or Jehovah's Witnesses. Certainly these people are usually well practised in the art of public speaking and can be guaranteed to make members think about religion even if they don't intend to put it into practice.

Consider the postmaster who could tell you about the workings of the post office and a bank manager about his world of finance. The Ratepayers Association, the Chamber of Commerce and local consumer groups are likely to welcome enquiries and the opportunity to publicize their work. Certainly local branches of charitable societies such as The Spastics, The National Association for Mental Health, The Red Cross and others will be willing to tell you about their organizations.

Find out from the library about other societies which exist in your area. Why not invite a specialist from the gliding association if you have one, the archaeological society, or a demonstrator from the keep fit class? What about judo, domestic poultry keeping, philately, music, yoga, chrysanthemums, photography and other clubs in your area which members might like to hear about?

Don't forget the police who supply speakers on various facets of their work including drug addiction, driving do's and don'ts, burglaries and safety first. And there is the editor of your newspaper and other journalists, the Gas and Electricity Boards who provide a wide range of talks and demonstrations and architects who may enlighten members on town and country planning as well as on house plans and conversions. Finally in this list come British Railways, river authorities and for those near the coast—port and harbour authorities.

A very important task for speaker finders is to make a study of local newspapers so that they are up to date with the local people who are making news and to keep a record for future use. Consider all the items of possible interest which you might put to good use in the form of speakers for your club. Here are some of the announcements from my local newspaper to give you some ideas.

'Mr Peter Heyworth, the Arts Master at Southbridge Grammar School, has recently returned from America where he has spent the last year on an exchange visit.'

'Mrs Betty Wakefield, a prominent member of the Southbridge Floral Art Society, has been awarded third prize in the Ideal Homes Flower Arrangement Competition Exhibition at Olympia.'

'The Citizen's Advice Bureau has opened a new branch at Church House, Yard Way, Southbridge.'

'Mr Brian Kershaw, manufacturer, of Kershaws Ltd, has invented an alarm for housebound invalids to use when needing help.'

'Miss Betty Granstead, aged seventeen, has been awarded the first prize at the Royal Academy of Dramatic Art for the best pupil of the year.'

'Miss Mary Leck has returned from spending three years nursing the Eskimos in a Lapland outpost.'

'Mr Percival Haynes, the well known expert on ceramics, has been appointed Assistant Editor to the Monthly Guide to Antique Collecting.'

All notable personalities can be contacted by writing to the newspaper office, or by looking them up in the telephone or street directory available at the library or general post office.

Another useful source of information in the local press is reports of the activities of other societies. (One can usually enquire discreetly from one of the members if their speakers were lively and interesting.) This method should not be employed all the time though, as it lacks imagination and takes away the individuality of a club.

Assuming you have exhausted all the possibilities described, where else can you turn? Look through the classified list of subscribers in the yellow pages section of all telephone directories. Many firms and organizations can be approached direct for speakers and some are willing to conduct tours of members round their premises as well. Local Chambers of Commerce are often able to supply information on those who offer these opportunities.

Nation-wide commercial firms

Many popular nation-wide commercial firms also give talks to clubs in various parts of Britain. I am not giving a list of these for the following reasons:—

1 Often they only operate within a certain radius of London or other large towns.

2 Many insist upon an audience of a certain size. (This can sometimes be overcome by arranging a joint meeting with another society.)

3 Sometimes they are booked up a very long time ahead.

4 Policies change. For instance, a firm may decide to promote a certain product and run a sales drive. At that time the firm is prepared to send out demonstrators to bring it to the notice of the public by speaking to organizations. The item in question may be a complete failure

or become an immediate success. Either way the need for its continued promotion in this manner has ceased.

5 Stringent economies have caused many firms to restrict demonstrations exclusively to schools and domestic science students.

Nevertheless, there are many other commercial firms, information centres, marketing boards and charitable bodies who *are* reliable. From time to time, popular women's magazines issue lists of speakers which give names of firms and organizations willing to accept bookings. These can be supplied to readers on request.

Meetings with a difference

Why not vary the rigid pattern of meetings sometimes? Hold a Better Driving Evening with a qualified instructor giving a short talk, and follow it up with a panel of motoring experts answering members' questions. A competition could be arranged beforehand for the best safety slogan to be judged on the night. A summer meeting could be held in a member's garden, or one could be organized on the lines of *Woman's Hour* with brief talks on a number of subjects. Speakers can usually be drawn from the club members.

Often a society has a great deal of talent within it and members can be approached to give the main talk if they have special knowledge and skills. Perhaps their husbands, wives, relations or acquaintances are qualified to speak on appropriate subjects too. If you know there are some members skilled in a particular craft, arrange demonstrations to take place as an added attraction from time to time. Techniques can be explained giving examples such as making mosaics with stones and shells, mending a fuse, bee keeping or life saving. This all helps to open up new channels of thought and interest to somebody.

The other evening a club I belong to asked each member to prepare a three minute talk on a subject of their choice.

Some spoke about their careers, others of humorous past incidents, or how they solved a domestic problem. We were surprised to hear the many different ideas, talents and interests put forward. A shared experience is a step towards new understanding of a person and there is many a bright light hidden under a bushel which can be discovered in this way.

Why not plan a series of three or four meetings with a variation on a single theme? For instance, take a country and explore its customs, history, education, food and geography. Local travel agents could be invited to describe holidays to the country in question, perhaps illustrated with transparencies, and the staff of nearby colleges approached to supply a speaker to cover the educational or geographical side of the subject. Why not ask a number of different charitable organizations to tell you about their work, or take careers or any other subject which can be viewed from a variety of angles?

Vote of thanks

I cannot finish this chapter without bringing up the matter of how to thank the speaker. This task seems to worry so many people who are called upon to do it, plunging the victim into such a panic that he or she is unable even to concentrate on the content of the talk. This is a pity because one of the most effective ways to thank a speaker is to refer to something which has been said.

If you know in advance that you are going to give a vote of thanks, do a little research and find out where the speaker comes from and exactly what his job entails. He may have written books on the subject or achieved something in a competitive field in which case you could refer to these facts, provided they were not mentioned in the introduction.

If you have been given no warning and are asked just before the talk begins or even after it has begun, as often happens, grab a pencil and a piece of paper and jot down anything said which strikes you as particularly interesting, or of practical use, or is new or amusing. With luck and some quick thinking you should be able to relate one of these incidents to something in your own, or the club's experiences. If you know the speaker personally, mention some particularly nice anecdote from the past, but don't reminisce too sentimentally. Once I did this and the speaker promptly burst into tears!

Finally, what to do if the speaker lets you down and rings up shortly before the meeting to say he can't come. Even in the best run clubs this disaster sometimes occurs. Think of past local speakers who have been popular, who have a wide range of interests and who might be willing to fall in with an emergency talk. Consider talented husbands, wives, children, friends and members who might also help out.

Why not build up a set of tranparencies of club activities that have taken place over the years and keep them ready to be shown as an emergency programme? Most clubs boast a member capable of taking photographs and the cost can be subsidized by club funds. Memorable events, exhibits, outings, visitors of importance or summer fund raising functions can all be recorded.

Perhaps there will be no warning. The first hint of disaster will come from the secretary's anxious glances at the clock and the firmly closed entrance door. Turn quickly to the next chapter for impromptu suggestions for all forms of audience participation.

Chapter 2

Joining in

'My biggest problem in running this club,' said a secretary recently, 'is getting shy members to come forward and join in any kind of discussion. They turn up week after week and listen passively to the speaker, yet never ask questions or enter into the conversation afterwards.'

Does this statement apply to some of the members of your club too? And do the same extroverts do all the talking whenever a point of view is required? How can the reticent be encouraged to come forward and take an active part in affairs?

A chance to chat is always appreciated because this helps members to know each other's backgrounds, tastes and problems. The act of swopping experiences not only brings understanding but it gives everybody something to talk about next time they meet. The more members voice their opinions, the better they will come to know each other. And then down come the barriers of shyness, age, class, suspicion and pride, and problems can be shared and seen in their true perspective.

On the whole, many people would like to take part in a more formal discussion and to be involved personally, but so often lack the courage to do so. They can be encouraged to contribute and communicate their thoughts and impressions if the subject matter is appropriate and presented in an attractive way, perhaps as an informal discussion, a debate or quiz, a brains trust or a more serious social study.

Selecting a subject
How does one set about choosing a subject to discuss? An idea practised by many general recreational clubs to help

select the most suitable topic and to ensure that members'
interests are served in the best possible way, is to compile
an interests register. A list is drawn up of all the subjects
which organizers *think* may appeal. It can include cultural
and leisure activities, scientific, technological, political,
educational and so on, and more can be added as they
present themselves. Members can be asked to tick the ones
they favour and from this a very useful guide will be available
to organizers.

Nobody would pretend that it's easy to pick the one subject
that will strike a sympathetic chord in everybody, but it is
the job of organizers to keep their ears to the ground, to be
aware of, and to know about members' difficulties, hopes,
ambitions and leisure activities. Much depends too upon the
particular phase of life through which members are passing.
In the case of a women's club, 'Starting a play-group' will
rouse the most tongue-tied mother to action if she has four
children under five, but the woman of forty will probably
not even bother to come to the meeting. But a mother whose
children are grown up and about to leave home will turn up
when there's to be a discussion on 'Part-time work in our
area'. Only by carefully tailoring the choice of subject
matter to the interests and needs of members can one hope
to shake them out of their lethargy.

Here to begin with are a few guide lines to help organizers
who are looking for general ideas and although a number of
them will not be suitable for your particular club, perhaps
they will spark off ideas.

Watch the main headlines of the newspapers for the
current news of the day. It might be 'Factory farming',
'Capital punishment' or 'Is this generation going to the
dogs?' but each issue will give food for thought. Study the
colour supplements which contain excellent surveys of such
items as 'Sleep and dreams', 'The permissive society' or
'Books and people who make them'. These supplements

usually offer a great deal of information and suggestions for further investigation and reading. Scan the *Radio Times* and *TV Times* and listen to radio talks, watch television documentaries, interviews and other similar programmes which provide serious subject matter. Buy *The Listener* if it contains the publication of a talk which might be used for discussion.

Find out what courses are running at the local colleges of further education. If a subject seems suitable for discussion or debate, ask the tutor if he would start it off. 'What is suitable reading matter for children' might be introduced by a lecturer in English, or 'The problems of a mixed marriage' by a sociologist.

Read the local newspapers for particular issues at stake in the district. For instance, is there a clash of opinion about the new caravan site destined for allocation to the gypsies? This caused much heated argument at a discussion in our club recently because a number of gypsy caravans had settled on the green outside a member's home. As she said, 'Why should *they* be allowed to camp there for months at a time when friends of mine who put up their tent to sleep in one summer weekend were ordered off the same day?'! Councillors could be invited to this sort of meeting to air their views and add grist to the mill.

Collecting information

Local societies may stimulate further ideas and help you collect information to chair a discussion. For instance, if an airport is being built or extended nearby and the noise affects the area, the secretary of the society for the prevention of the development will be only too pleased to come and give his point of view. Some members may want to see the airport grow and their opinions will provide a new angle.

Several members might be persuaded to study a subject sufficiently to introduce it for discussion if they know where to get facts. Almost any subject under consideration can be opened up by a visit to the library where bibliographies may suggest ideas if the books in stock yield nothing suitable. And the *British Yearbook of Associations* (available in larger libraries) contains addresses of all main societies in the country and a letter to the secretary (enclosing a stamped addressed envelope) will usually bring further information. Suppose you felt a discussion on 'Education—State or Independent' would be an appropriate subject to introduce to your society, then letters to the Department of Education and Science, the Society for the Abolition of Public Schools, the Association of Progressive Schools, the Independent Schools Movement and the Advisory Centre for Education may all be able to supply some informative literature. When writing, explain the project and give some idea of the particular aspects of your discussion. All these organizations are listed under subject headings as well as in alphabetical order, so it is a simple matter to trace the one most suited to your needs.

There is a wealth of information on both home and overseas affairs obtainable from the Central Office of Information (address Appendix) from the modest price of 4p a fact sheet. A free catalogue listing papers, pamphlets and fact sheets is available on a very wide range of subjects including *Social Services, Population, The Press* and *Town and Country Planning*.

Having decided upon the subject most likely to stimulate the interest of members, let us now turn to the actual running of what might loosely be termed 'audience participation'.

Discussions

There are many ways of holding a discussion, but all require that the chairman gives time beforehand to collecting information, facts, figures and books which are relevant to the subject. He or she can then introduce the subject to open the discussion and call on members to give further points of view. But this is not always successful because many people are too shy to speak on the spur of the moment. A more satisfactory method is to run one as follows.

The chairman selects a few members to be group leaders beforehand and briefs them on the main points to be discussed. The idea is that each will take charge of a small number of members who will then talk about the matter between themselves for about ten minutes.

The groups can be selected at the meeting by issuing lettered cards distributed at random so that after the chairman's opening address they can gather round their leaders. For instance, all those with cards beginning with A will assemble in one corner of the room for a discussion led by Mrs Jones, while B's will go to Mr Sargent, and so on.

After the talks have taken place, the leaders should summarize the opinions of their groups and the meeting is then thrown open to general discussion. The matter can finally be put to the vote or a motion passed if necessary.

Other forms of discussion

The interview
An outside visitor is introduced to the group with a specialized knowledge of a particular subject. Members should be asked previously to bring suitable questions. One can be briefed to begin the interview then others can join in the friendly cross-examination.

Buzz Groups
Sometimes there is a particular problem which is causing worry and concern within a club. Divide into buzz groups— i.e. into groups of about five people just where they sit. Present the problem and ask for ideas to solve it. Time allowed—six minutes! From the numbers of ideas voiced in the general relaxed chatter of a small group, four or five clear

lines of action will probably present themselves which can be acted upon while the interest is there.

The critics
Suggest to members prior to the meeting that they read a magazine, book, listen to a programme on radio or watch a television programme and then discuss their views about it.

Pot luck
Write a number of topics on small slips of paper and place in a hat. Each member draws one out and gives a two-minute impromptu talk on the subject. Such titles as 'My job', or 'What I did before I married' or 'It bores me' are easy to talk about on the spur of the moment.

If it happens that there is silence during the course of a discussion, a very simple way to help things along is to announce that there will be a break of two or three minutes. Members invariably turn to each other and pour out their reactions. This helps them to form their opinions and when the bell is rung tongues are loosened and the views and questions flow freely. So often one feels nervous of saying something which may sound absurd, but a quick reassurance from your neighbours that they feel the same too makes all the difference.

Of course, sometimes the boot is on the other foot and somebody just won't stop talking. We all know a Mr Somebody who once he gets on his hobby horse carries on and on. This calls for great tact on the part of the chairman who ideally should be able to pick up some particular point and break in quickly to say 'Mrs So and So is an expert on that subject, let's ask her what SHE thinks.' Some chairmen use a bell to ring after each speaker has gone on for three minutes, but on the whole, this tends to frighten others into not speaking at all.

Now let us turn to the more organized forms of audience participation.

Debates

Debates should ideally be run when there is a particular issue of importance at stake, whether at club, community, town, county or national level. There is usually some topic which is foremost in everybody's mind and alert organizers should be quick to spot what it is and put the plan into action. It need not necessarily form the entire part of a programme and if time runs out before all have had their say, announce that the debate will be continued as part of the next meeting. Suggest that in the meantime members examine their own opinions on the subject.

Debates can be run successfully in clubs of all sizes from a small group to a packed audience in a large hall. Basic requirements are a chairman and two speakers, one to put the motion and the other to oppose it. Supporting speakers can be appointed to provide more argument and add zest to the entertainment. Each will have their allotted time to speak which may be ten, five or two minutes, according to the time available. When the speakers have had their fill of demolishing their opponent's opinions, the audience may join in if they wish. But the vital thing is that whether the motion is being supported or opposed, definite opinions should be stated. It's no good sitting on the fence. For instance, our club held a debate recently on 'Is honesty the best policy?'. It was a great temptation to say 'Well, honesty is usually the best policy, but there are occasions when a little white lie is permissible.' Instead, each speaker had to come down heavily on one side or the other. Honesty IS the best policy because to build up trust and respect for yourself is so important and leads to a peaceful state of mind. Or, speaking the truth was often unkind and lost you friends and in the long run did more harm than good and was therefore NOT the best policy.

The chairman must hold the meeting firmly in hand. All opinions whether from official speakers or audience must be addressed to him, otherwise the whole thing can easily be reduced to a slanging match. A bell can be used on this type of occasion to terminate any members of the audience who voice their opinion for more than one or two minutes. It is also an advantage if the chairman can alternate the views of the audience—for or against the motion—but this is not always possible. When the general discussion is concluded, the chairman calls upon the opposer to reply. Finally the proposer sums up his veiws and has the last word.

The chairman then 'puts the question'. 'Will those in favour of the motion put up their hands?' 'Will those against the motion do the same?' The motion is carried or lost according to the result of the count.

The quiz contest

There are many types of entertainment which fall under this heading, but they are all run in a similar manner. In its simplest form, two teams comprised of four to eight people each, face each other and between them sits the question master. Another person is appointed judge, a second scores, and a third marks the passing of time allowed for answers, with the aid of a stopwatch and a bell or gong.

The chairman or question master must be 'on the ball' and able to encourage, discipline and generally hold the show together with flashes of wit and humour. He must also stop the audience from 'chipping in' with the answers before the team whose turn it is has had a chance to reply.

Ideas for questions can be compiled under various headings. General knowledge, handicrafts, local affairs, music, sport and so on. Questions can be taken straight from such paperback books as the BBC publication *Ask the Family*, price 25p, and others obtainable from most bookshops.

Inter-quiz contests

Top of the group contests, where societies challenge each

other over a period of time, are great fun. This is an excellent way to get around and make contact with other clubs in the neighbourhood. Members can exchange views and opinions, discuss problems of running a club and generally widen their horizons at the same time.

Brain games

Study radio and television programmes which offer endless scope for fresh ideas which can be adapted to suit a particular society. Examples which run from time to time are:—

My Word	A team quiz concerned with meanings and derivations of words, sources of quotations, etc.
My Music	The same as above but concerned with musical matters.
A Question of Sport *Quiz Ball*	Teams answer questions on sport.
So You Think You Know All About....	Teams of professionals and amateurs in a particular field compete in their knowledge of the facts. Audience can also keep individual scores.
Just a Minute	Contestants try to speak for a minute on a given subject without hesitation, repetition or deviation. Opponents challenge, score for upheld challenge and take over subject.
Call My Bluff	Members tell tall stories and the opposing team guesses whether they are true or false.
What's My Line	Panel tries to guess occupation of challengers. 'Yes' or 'No' answers only allowed.

Twenty Questions	Contestants try to guess identity of mystery objects in twenty questions or less.
Spelling Bee	Individuals or teams compete in skill in spelling.
Going For a Song	Experts and amateurs describe and date antiques.

Brains trusts and panels

The purpose of a brains trust is to open the minds of an audience to the lives which other people live and to share their opinions and knowledge. In order to ensure the success of running such an event, the right ingredients must be put into it.

The first task is to decide exactly what it is you want to produce. Is it to be an instructional or a purely entertaining brains trust? If the former, you will naturally go for the specialists in the particular subject you have chosen. If the latter, try to collect popular personalities who are prepared to talk about subjects the audience will understand and who can speak with authority on the problems that directly affect members of the audience. A church youth group in our town chose a panel of people representing each decade of life, the first being in his twenties and the last in his seventies. Each one was asked to state what he or she thought was wrong with teenagers today. Only one rule was imposed. 'No comment from the audience until the panel has finished giving their opinions.' Afterwards the flood gates were opened when teenagers gave their replies.

Another time, my husband who is a paediatrician, was a member of a panel with the local vicar, schoolmaster and a children's officer. The questions were submitted on subjects connected with bringing up children and audience participation was encouraged, which led to a very lively meeting.

It is almost always an advantage if members of a panel are

well known personalities in your district. Tremendous interest is shown by an audience if the local landowner is asked for his views on the law concerning abortion, but bring in an unknown marriage guidance counsellor from the next county and nobody really cares what he thinks.

When considering whom to ask to form the team, consult the editor of your local paper who is in the best position of all to recommend notable personalities in your town. Remember others in the community such as the mayor and his councillors (all used to public speaking), ministers of religion, headmasters, matrons, managing directors, bank managers and those engaged in the creative arts such as journalists, authors and musicians.

Although it is wise to choose a team who share a number of things in common, it is fatal if they all come from the same background and agree with each other about every issue which arises. Mix male and female, youth and age, the sophisticated and unsophisticated, the serious and frivolous, but do make sure that each person is a specialist in some sphere. Never mind if it's pop music, bee keeping, child welfare or sewage disposal. So long as he or she can speak well the audience will be enthralled to hear an expert expound upon his own subject. They will be even more delighted if, after giving a brilliant discourse on the technical theory of, say, a complicated computer, the same chap later has to admit to not having the faintest idea how to mend a fuse or grow wallflowers from seed. This is the essence of a successful brains trust.

Having settled the panel of speakers, how do you collect the questions? The chairman of the society should announce the forthcoming event well in advance so that members can consider appropriate questions to submit. Ask for them to be sent on a postcard or delivered beforehand if possible, then the question master can select the most suitable.

What sort of questions should be chosen? Librarians can

be helpful here because they have a very good idea of the subjects which interest the local population at any given time. But in general the rule to apply is 'Does it have direct application to the interests and activities of the audience?' One question should relate to the talents of each specialist and this can be followed by asking the opinions of the rest of the team on the subject. With luck, this will draw out their wit, humour and fury which all helps to keep the audience in a state of anticipation, wondering if the whole thing will finish in a stand-up fight.

Should the panel be allowed to read the questions before-hand to enable them to compose studied answers? Better not, say the experts, because it has the effect of robbing the entertainment of its spontaneity. Random questions and opinions from the audience can be welcomed and developed if they appear promising. And if the question master knows a certain member in the audience is an expert on any parti-cular point, he can all upon that person to speak. Here are a few final words of advice:—

1 Introduce each speaker with a build-up of his special attributes and experiences so that it makes it clear to the audience what subject he or she is an authority upon.
2 Make the first question simple enough for each member of the trust to answer. Bring on a serious question fairly early as the audience is most alert during the first half hour.
3 Introduce a light hearted question after a serious session.
4 Keep the questions short, simple and easy to understand, but if possible designed to provoke.
5 Save a few special questions for the conclusion which should require only instant replies. The last one is the most important of all and should call for an opinion from each member of the trust which will leave the audience with something to think about.
6 Prepare at least twenty questions for an hour's session.

Chapter 3

Recreation

A most important factor in the life of any society is for
members to get to know one another. There should be time
set aside at each meeting for enjoyment, to sit back and
laugh, to talk and make friends. It's good to get out and
about on outings too, and visit new places and things, meet
new people and experience different pleasures. The provision of social events at club headquarters from time to
time offers members a welcome break from more serious
activities. Recreation, whether in the form of outings,
excursions, parties or socials, offers opportunities for
'letting go' and meeting fellow members in a relaxed atmosphere.

Outings

Let's begin this chapter by considering some of the day
excursions and outings which societies might like to plan.
Of course, a great deal depends upon the situation of the
society, but here are some general ideas to help organizers:—

1 Consult the many guides issued annually with up-to-date
information. Public libraries stock many brochures and
pamphlets. Coach companies produce leaflets offering
attractive day outings and British Railways run special day
excursions to places of scenic beauty or to special events.

2 Visits can be made to dozens of stately homes, gardens,
museums, castles and other places of interest. *Historic
Houses, Castles and Gardens in Great Britain and Ireland*

and *Museums and Galleries in Great Britain and Ireland,* both published by Index Publications at 25p each, are excellent informative books available from bookstalls and booksellers.

Special events of all kinds, sports, traditional ceremonies, exhibitions, town carnivals and other functions are held up and down the country throughout the year. County magazines and local and county newspapers give notices of forthcoming events in an area so that organizers can make arrangements well in advance. The British Travel Association (address page 121) produces a monthly guide entitled *Coming Events in Britain* which covers events for the next three months and contains information on highlights for subsequent months.

3   Spend a day afloat on a canal, river, lake or on the sea. In the London area Thames Launches Ltd. (address page 124) supply vessels for private hire with meals provided according to requirements. Enquire locally to canal, river, harbour or port authorities where similar opportunities may be available for your society.

4   Outings to theatres, cinemas, concerts, pageants, dance, music and drama festivals and other public performances are always popular. Local amateur theatrical productions (and sometimes professional) offer reduced rates to parties usually on Monday or Tuesday evenings.

Outings to firms, factories and organizations of various kinds can sometimes be arranged if planned well in advance (see page 27). Visits to watch sound radio or television performances enacted before an audience in most parts of Britain can be booked by writing to BBC Ticket Units (addresses page 121). Indicate the programme you would like to see, plus two alternative programmes, and enclose a stamped addressed envelope.

Organizing an outing
Having decided upon the place to visit, how is the outing to
be organized? Assuming transport is required, the obvious
answer is to arrange for a coach to collect members, deposit
them at the destination and return them safely home
afterwards.

1 Find out first how many members show interest in a
   proposed outing. Providing there is a reasonable number,
   contact coach companies (see yellow pages of local
   telephone directories) to enquire about dates, size of
   coaches available (e.g. can they provide the right sized
   coach whether for eight persons or forty) and the
   approximate prices. Select the company most able to
   supply the necessary requirements.
2 Fix the most suitable date with members at the next
   meeting and check with the coach company. Take
   bookings and a non-returnable deposit.
3 Pass round a notice for members who want to go to sign
   their names. State the times, venue and the inclusive cost
   of seat, lunch, tea, supper, coffees, etc., and the tip to
   the driver (approximately 15%). Do not include the
   entrance fee to stately homes and other similar places as
   cost varies according to numbers.
4 It is advisable if possible, to see hotel or restaurant
   managers where the main meal is taken in order to check
   arrangements, especially if there are handicapped people
   in the party. Levels of floors, toilet facilities and also
   possible restrictions on children should all be investigated.
5 All money should be paid in by members at least seven
   days prior to the outing. If members cancel after this
   date, they must find their own replacement or lose the
   money.
6 Arrange for two people to share the organization of the
   outing in case one falls ill.

7   Check coach booking and confirm meal booking in writing at least two days before the outing is to take place.
8   Try to arrange for 'comfort' stops after about two and a half hours on both outward and return journeys.

Organizers themselves should arrive well ahead of time on the day of the outing in order to check the passengers and also to give final directions to the driver. On one occasion an outing was arranged to take a party of old people from a home to visit a stately castle and garden. The organizers arrived at the arranged time for departure, armed with a sumptuous picnic tea, only to discover the coach and passengers had already departed! The driver had taken it upon himself to organize his own mystery tour and the old people never did get their cucumber sandwiches and strawberry tarts.

It is also important to count everybody each time the coach is re-boarded because it is very easy indeed to leave somebody behind. This did actually happen to a member of our society. Despite offering profuse apologies the next morning, the organizers have never been forgiven. Before letting people out of the coach be sure they all know the time they must return to it, but an ultimatum can be issued stating that after a certain time the coach will leave.

Social events

Now let us turn to enjoying ourselves at social events run on our own home ground, perhaps at the village hall, a member's house or at a venue hired for the occasion. In my previous book *Be My Guest* I have described all kinds of imaginative party themes suitable for clubs and societies. I do not intend to repeat these ideas here, but rather to concentrate on the ways in which organizers of social occasions can cut down on expenditure of those vital commodities—

time and money. At the same time I have included some suggestions for making the party go with a swing.

Organizing a social occasion
Decide the following:—

1 What kind of function is it going to be? Large, small or medium, formal or informal.
2 The date and times.
3 How much money can be allowed for expenditure or is the cost to be covered entirely by the price of the ticket.
4 The publicity. It can be by:—
        (a) invitation
        (b) programmes
        (c) posters and advertisements

Decide upon the wording and as soon as the tickets are in hand, distribute them to members and ask for payment at the same time.

Whom to invite
Are you going to allow members to bring guests and if so, how many? If the event is likely to be very popular it may be necessary to restrict entry by allowing one guest per person. On the other hand you may wish to extend invitations to other clubs in the vicinity to whom you may be affiliated, or with whom you have a common bond. Many societies invite the handicapped, old people and other sections of their community to share a social occasion. This invariably gives as much pleasure to those giving the party as it does to the guests.

If you are planning to invite another club or society make sure you have the co-operation of your members. There is no more dismal sight than that of a visiting club sitting in isolated rows talking to each other. It is up to the host club to detail their own members, one to each visitor, to look after and introduce them to others.

Many societies use the personal label system for all their big functions. (Obtainable from most good stationers' shops). These serve an excellent purpose apart from introducing stranger to stranger. They refresh the memory of members who have forgotten each other's names—something which happens all too often! Print the letters in block capitals as large as possible, otherwise they can only be read by peering at close range.

Methods of catering
Who is going to provide the all important festive spread? Wealthy societies who can afford professional caterers can skip the next few paragraphs, but for those clubs who must provide their own catering for social occasions here are some suggestions:—

The committee provides
This is probably the most popular and accepted method of providing a meal for a club's social occasion. Each member of the catering committee provides one section of the menu. For instance, one will be responsible for roasting all the chicken pieces, frying pounds of sausages, or baking a ham. Another supervises the cooking of potatoes in their jackets, another the sliced tomatoes and cucumbers and yet another the cole slaw salad, the sliced beetroot and so on. Fruit salad can be obtained in bulk tins and fresh cream adds the festive touch if it can be afforded. Rolls, butter, cheese and biscuits, coffee and other drinks must also be considered. I need hardly add that each person involved in preparations should keep careful accounts of expenditure.

It is often difficult to gauge the exact amount of food which is required, but it is wise to err on the side of generosity. If anything is left over when the meal is finished it can often be sold off to members, but not always. A friend of mine thought she had carefully calculated the amount of spaghetti required to feed thirty club members on spaghetti bolognese. She had followed the instructions on the packet, but they were wildly out of proportion and a mountain of spaghetti was left over. It lay around the kitchen heaped in saucepans, on draining boards, blocking up the sinks and spilling over every available surface. The moral is, before cooking a dish in bulk, try it out on the family first.

Bring a 'sweet or savoury' for a buffet
Each member attending an event of this nature brings a sweet or savoury dish which is enough for herself and her guests. Naturally organizers will work out quantities carefully, but remember that more savouries are consumed per head in comparison to 'sweet' dishes. Two thirds of the total number of members should bring a savoury dish. Suitable items are sausage rolls, sausages on sticks, vol-au-vents, sandwiches, small meat patties or chicken legs, followed by fruit jellies, trifles and fruit salad.

An extension of this idea is for some members to bring enough for four in a covered dish—hot or cold. This can vary from Paella, Quiche Lorraine, steak and kidney pie or kedgeree and so on, followed by any kind of dessert such as flans, crumbles, tarts or mousse. All savoury items are set on one table and desserts on another. Everybody is allowed one *teaspoonful* of each item. The first comers must remember the last comers if there is to be fair shares for all.

Hostess for each table
Another method of catering is to appoint a host and hostess or two hostesses to each trestle table seating ten people. They are responsible for providing the dessert (main course is prepared by the committee), laying up the table and doing the flowers. This shares out the preparatory work and creates variety and interest.

Take-away food
Most towns have Chinese and Indian restaurants providing a take-away food service. Organizers can negotiate in advance for any number of hot meals to be ready packed for collection at a certain specified time. Many restaurants will undertake delivery as well, and in my experience have been most reliable.

Investigate other take-away foods in the locality apart from the usual fish, chicken and meat pies with chips. Shops providing a wider range of cooked meals are opening up everywhere. We have one which sells ready-to-serve goulash, beef stroganoff and other dishes and the cost works out considerably cheaper than hiring caterers or going out to a restaurant.

The professional or semi-professional cook
Sometimes it happens that a member of a society is a competent or even professional cook. If he or she is willing, why not make use of this talent? Domestic science teachers and pupils are often pleased to do this sort of thing for experience and they are usually capable of producing excellent party food. Although it will have to be paid for, the price will not be so high as it would be for the services of a professional caterer. Enquiries can be made at local colleges and schools.

Entertainment
When the meal is over and the efficient committee members have removed the dirty dishes and the last coffee cups have been cleared away—what next? Whatever the function, whether small, large, grand or unsophisticated, nothing gives more pleasure than an entertainment put on by members themselves. It can be anything from singing a few old time music songs to giving a performance of bell ringing, fencing, juggling or anything else which displays members' talents. There are a number of suggestions contained in Chapter 5,

but if nothing can be produced in this line—what other plans can be devised to keep the party going?

Games

At the mention of the word 'games', most sophisticated club members throw up their hands in horror. Other still carry on regardless, playing their traditional favourites and getting more fun out of them than anything else. Members can be asked at a previous meeting to bring any games they have at home, such as darts, bagatelle, table soccer or roulette. Books on games can be obtained from libraries which will give further ideas.

However, panel or quiz games are now much in fashion and seem to be acceptable to all. Variations of this pastime can be adapted to the particular interests of members and guests. (See Chapter 2.)

Dancing

The straightforward dance is probably the most acceptable form of entertainment for a number of people of mixed sexes. Whether it takes the form of strict tempo, the Blues, jazz combos, beat groups, Latin American or a pop group, will depend entirely upon the tastes and pockets of club members. Anything required can be supplied by the Entertainment Agents' Association (address page 122), who will put organizers in touch with local agents. This applies to cabaret, pop stars and all other acts.

'Disco' with special lighting effects and the top fifty discs is becoming very popular. Mobile Discotheque Sounds Systems (address page 124) can provide disc jockeys, equipment, special lighting or live groups if required.

Coming down the scale, bands in your area can be contacted by enquiring at town halls and through the advertisements in local newspapers. Sometimes amateur groups run by sixth form schoolboys are the most 'with it' of all, but remember that personal recommendation is the safest way to ensure satisfaction all round.

Other types of dancing are also greatly enjoyed by some societies on social occasions. Country dancing (square or folk) can be organized with the help of the nearest branch of The English Folk Dance and Song Society (address page 122). One of their members can be invited to play the role of 'caller' on the night.

Our club ran an event of this nature last summer in a large barn belonging to a member. The three-piece band performed on top of a picturesque old wagon. Cartwheels and sheaves of corn made a striking decoration against the old walls and oak rafters, across which hung enormous cobwebs. Birds fluttered in the high vaulted roof. Members wore old fashioned country smocks, Victorian dresses, bonnets and shawls and the dances were led by the experienced caller. The steps were easy to follow and simple enough to be understood by the uninitiated. Cold ham, salad, potato mayonnaise and fruit pie were provided by the committee and each couple brought their own bottle of wine to drink. The inclusive cost of the ticket?—50p.

Other forms of entertainment
The showing of films (see Chapter 5), organizing a sing-song by issuing duplicated song sheets, playing bingo, whist, or running a beetle drive, all provide possibilities for entertainment. A 'gaming' party with roulette, pontoon and black jack can be played, or a 'saloon bar' evening can be organized with dominoes, shove ha'penny, draughts and marbles.

Competitions can be introduced with success on some occasions. At a party given recently for a number of old people's clubs, a silver tray was awarded to the club which gave the best performance of any kind on stage. This was so enjoyed that it is to be an annual event in the future.

Don't overlook the fun of dressing up. Fancy dress parties

break the ice quicker than anything else. A successful one we ran at Christmas had the provocative title 'Tarts and Vicars'. Finding the right clothes was simplicity itself—just a dog collar for the men and slinky dresses, plenty of jewellery, false eyelashes and other appropriate touches for the girls. This is an important point nowadays when time is in short supply. But even if guests only wear a hat or a mask, it gives people a good excuse to start a friendly conversation.

This is your life—a farewell tribute

To finish this chapter, here is a most charming idea which has been carried out with great success in recent years. When a member of long standing retires or perhaps moves to another part of the country, his or her colleagues conspire in the greatest secrecy to produce a special surprise party, in the form of—This is Your Life.

Of course it requires a good deal of preparation and the whole affair must be worked out like a military operation. The help of husbands, wives and friends must be enlisted to make tape recordings of those people who cannot be present on the night of the party. This can be done by arranging for these absent friends to ring well in advance of the date on an evening when a tape recorder is fixed up by the telephone ready to record their personal message.

Guests must arrive at a specific time and the chairman begins the meeting in the ordinary way dealing with the business. When this is finished, the microphone crackles into life and the chairman's voice announces—'Mary Smith—This is Your Life'.

The content of the rest of the evening will depend entirely upon the incidents and past events which have happened in your society. The various occasions should be recalled in sequence, with appropriate tape recordings from the members who took part in them but could not be there, or by the personal appearance of those brought back especially for the party.

Recordings of music, songs or excerpts from plays or anything else which holds special memories of the past can be played. Humorous anecdotes can be retold and appropriate gifts, photographs and mementos presented when the opportunity arises.

Can you think of a better way to show friendship and gratitude to somebody who has given years of loyal service to a club?

Chapter 4

Organizing an exhibition or show

Why bother? Is it worth the mental effort and sheer physical hard work which the committee and many members will have to put into mounting an exhibition of any kind? The answer from those who have already done so will certainly be, 'It's worth it. Go ahead and have a go!'

Apart from the fun and excitement of putting on an exhibition it shows the public what your society can do and it probably recruits more members than any other method. It also provides a common meeting ground for other clubs in the district with similar interests. Ideas can be swopped, trends discussed and new suggestions can be adopted in the future.

When a club decides to put on a show for the public, it calls for the co-operation of almost every single member. Although the first reaction is usually 'No. I couldn't possibly enter an exhibit myself', it is up to the clever organizers to draw out talents which may have lain dormant in members for years. Even if they cannot be persuaded to exhibit, they can be roped in to help with publicizing, putting up the stands, catering or some other vital task.

It would be an impossibility to put down methods for every kind of exhibition. But whether the items on show are photographs, fruits and vegetables, cage birds, model railways, amateur paintings, flower arrangements, handicrafts or anything else, certain basic items concerning the organization and running of the event are the same.

Bear in mind right from the beginning that the word exhibition can be interpreted freely. Other appropriate attractions can be introduced such as a gardening quiz or a brains trust at a flower, fruit and vegetable show or a demonstration of cake icing at a produce show. Exhibitions of crafts put on by women's organizations often include such extras as a mannequin parade, choir singing, performances of music, prose and poetry readings, as well as actual demonstrations of some of the crafts on show. These might be weaving, basket making, toy making, millinery, lampshade making and so on. Many exhibitions run for several days and subsidiary items of entertainment can vary daily, all adding to the fun and excitement of the whole project.

Appointing a committee
Whatever the reasons for putting on your show, the first task will be to select a committee whose numbers will naturally depend upon the size of the function. As a rough guide, the following can be appointed:—
  1   A Chairman
  2   A Secretary
  3   A Treasurer
  4   A Schedule Secretary
  5   A Press Officer
  6   A Staging and Display Officer
  7   A Catering Officer
Sub-committees can be formed if helpers are numerous.

Contact the local authority at an early stage if the object of the show is to edify or instruct. Town councillors are often proud of what their ratepayers can produce and will try to help.

Choosing the date
A good time to hold an exhibition is from the beginning of March to the end of May and late September to mid-November, but take care that it does not clash with another function in the area. Visit the local newspaper office and look

up the copies issued for the corresponding dates of the previous year and see what functions took place then. Ring up the organizer concerned and ask him what date he has in mind for events during the coming year. Also consult the Town Diary which can be seen at the Town Hall.

Venue

Naturally the choice will depend upon the size of the show, whether a hall is already available anyway, and the financial state of the society. Easy accessibility is most important. Ample car parking, a bus service, possibly catering facilities, the distance from the shops and other factors must all be taken into account.

Financing the exhibition

It is wise to raise some money to finance the project beforehand (see Chapter 6).

Some societies make a small charge to each exhibitor. The public can also be charged an entrance fee and extra for demonstrations. But it is preferable to raise money in other ways and this can be done to a large extent by running stalls, a raffle, a tombola and so on. Sometimes exhibitors are willing to sell their crafts and if this is so, arrangements can be made beforehand for a percentage of the sales to be retained by the society.

The theme

It helps to make a show more interesting if it has a special title so that all the entries can be tied to one theme. 'The Heritage of our County' is a popular and easy to depict title for exhibitions of women's handicrafts, and help and advice can be sought from librarians and historians. The cookery section can display dishes of the county, the wines be made from local ingredients, the flower arrangements depict the county's history, and dolls can be dressed in traditional costumes. Other products or specialities of a county can be displayed according to what form they take. Our town produces a famous brand of leather gloves and at a recent exhibition held by a church group, items were provided to mount a display on how skins are cured. This led on appropriately enough to an exhibit of the work of members who had attended the club's glove making classes.

Consider also topical events when searching for a title and theme for your exhibition such as the moon landings, the boom in holiday travel, the age of leisure or 'Into 197—'. The festivals and seasons of the year give rise to many possibilities which will inspire members to get cracking. A 'Spring Again Exhibition', 'A Show for Mother's Day', 'Easter Roundabout' or 'Leisure and Pleasure' for an autumn hobbies show are all titles which will catch the public's eye.

It may also be possible to choose a title to tie in with a national sporting occasion, a film, book, popular television feature or serial, depending on the nature of your exhibition and the type of contents to be displayed. By using imagination and ingenuity it is not difficult to adapt the ideas and talents of members to fit the theme once the enthusiasm is there.

Framing the schedule

Experienced organizers know that this is the heart and soul of any exhibition. It must be compiled as soon as the date and place have been decided so that all exhibitors have several weeks to contemplate the classes they wish to enter. Whether they are to be competitive or non-competitive, or some of each, will depend upon the individual society. But whatever is decided, members should be encouraged to enter as many exhibits as possible.

Well in advance of the exhibition, try to arrange for special talks or demonstrations to be given by experts in the subjects chosen for the schedule, particularly if minority interests are to be catered for. For instance, our Flower Arrangement Society organized an exhibition with one class entitled 'An Arrangement of dried plant material suitable for a Guy Fawkes Supper Party'. An expert had given a demonstration to the club some time before giving examples of dried flower arrangements. This naturally inspired members and gave them confidence to enter the class in the show.

A copy of the exhibition schedule must be sent to each member and should include the following:

1 Name of association. Date. Time and place of exhibition and the name of whoever is to open it.
2 The titles of classes of entry.
3 Name, address, telephone number of the secretary and a list of other officials.
4 Details concerning the latest date and payment of entrance fee for entering the classes.
5 A list of prizes.
6 The date and time for staging.
7 The time when exhibits may be removed and the time of closing.
8 The amount of space allotted for each exhibit or group of exhibits.
9 Whom to contact for further information and where to send the enclosed entry form.

Further rules and regulations applicable to your society and its individual needs should be stated clearly on this notice. Remember, a schedule cannot be too explicit.

Exhibitors who enter classes for competition must be given a card on arrival numbered on one side, with the exhibitor's name and address on the other. These will be placed beside the exhibits with the name sides down. Stewards and the show secretary must be present during staging time to direct operations and answer queries.

Judges

Consult local newspaper editors and librarians for suitable experts such as authors, professors and other authorities who may live in the district and be willing to offer their services. For example, veterinary surgeons make good judges of pet shows, domestic science teachers are experts on cookery, art masters on paintings, parks superintendents on flowers and plants and journalists on essays. If you are still not satisfied, write to editors of national magazines specializing in the subjects of your exhibition and they may be able to suggest somebody suitable living within striking distance of your town.

Prizes

Local tradesmen may be willing to offer prizes in return for an advertisement in the schedule. Often firms who have a vested interest in the particular exhibits will donate prizes too. For instance, glue or balsa wood manufacturers might offer prizes for a model engineering exhibition, or horticultural firms give gift boxes of seeds at a flower and vegetable show. Addresses and names of directors of firms in this country can be obtained from the reference rooms of public libraries. Local shops selling items required for producing exhibits can also be approached for a prize.

Publicity

Whether the show is to be set up in a tin hut, a converted barn or the town hall, the press officer's job is to make it known, along with the date, time and other details. Approach local newspapers four weeks in advance (see page 98) and send letters or leaflets giving details of the event to the following:—

> The Chamber of Commerce
> The Trades Council
> The Council of Churches

Residents Associations
Head Teachers
Parent Teacher Associations
Chamber of Trade
Council of Social Service
Ratepayers Associations
Community Associations
Clubs and Societies in the district

Further information on methods of publicity can be found in Chapters 8 and 9.

Staging the exhibition

There are a number of books which can be consulted on this very large subject notably, *Window Display* by G. Fazakerley (EUP) and *Display Technique* by H. Muscott (Mills and Boon, now out of print but sometimes obtainable through public libraries). But visit other exhibitions held in the area, talk to organizers and ask their advice.

To conclude this chapter, I give a brief outline of how to stage an exhibition. Naturally, this will vary a great deal according to the type of exhibit, but in the main, the basic rules are as follows:—

1 Make a plan of the proposed exhibition on graph paper using coloured paper for each display in scale. Try to use variety in the lay-out by the use of island displays, semi-circular arrangements and grouped exhibits. Leave space for demonstrations and sideshows and room for the public to move freely by planning a traffic flow.

2 Each display should have a focal point upon which attention is riveted with the aid of a spotlight if possible. Consider borrowing items from shops, embassies, tourist offices, firms and other organizations. Cardboard boxes can be up-ended and used one on top of the other to make platforms and stands to create the illusion of depth.

3   An overall colour scheme makes great impact and lifts a show into the professional class. Crepe paper is obtainable in quantity cheaply from Barnums (address page 121).

4   Textures are all important and set the right atmosphere. For example, if luxury is to be depicted, the stand can be draped in velvet, silk or satin, with corrugated paper columns. For an outdoor subject, grass matting, canvas, natural wood and rope will help to produce the right effect.

5   Backgrounds and floors need to be considered and be appropriate to the theme. Wallpaper patterned with bricks, a seascape, flowers or other suitable subjects can be used and, scattered on the floor, appropriate items such as pebbles, sand or fur rugs.

6   Silhouettes and shapes are most effective and can be constructed from cardboard, plastic sheeting, cartridge paper, expanded polystyrene, wire, wire netting, straw, rope and other materials. A simple method of producing an outline is to trace it from a large picture or photograph.

7   Prepare short, pithy captions on cardboard telling the onlookers what the display is about. Good, clear lettering is essential. If in difficulty, use a stencil or letraset.

8   Leave space between each item or group of items. Nothing destroys effect more than overcrowding.

9   Arrange for the last exhibit to be an informative display giving details of club membership and its activities and put up a notice board giving a list of forthcoming events.

It is worth while appointing hostesses to greet guests as they come in the door and to ask them to sign a visitors' book. From this a useful list of people interested in the activities of a society can be used in the future—perhaps to invite them to attend other club events or to increase membership.

Chapter 5

Producing entertainments

All those who have taken part in the production of an entertainment of any kind usually agree unanimously upon one thing. 'It was such fun', they say. From the leading lady down to the programme seller, a sense of excitement seems to take hold of everybody which makes the hard work put into the project worth all the effort.

What is it about putting on a show which is so rewarding? One of the main reasons is because it brings together a number of people from different backgrounds and throws them into a new and shared experience. Secondly, the entertainment is greatly appreciated by the members who watch it. Often a club party or a special social occasion falls flat after the meal and tails off miserably as people drift home. But what a different atmosphere there is when a performance of some kind is going to be staged.

In this chapter, it would not be possible to tackle the whole subject of amateur dramatics in detail. I have merely endeavoured to put down some guide lines, to throw out ideas and suggest further reading to help those who are contemplating putting on some simple kind of entertainment. The important thing is for members to enjoy what they're doing and maybe just play or poetry reading around a member's fireside will give complete satisfaction. Others will be more ambitious, but if the producer and cast can keep a sense of humour along with the ability to adapt and improvise— all will be well.

What type of show?
What type of entertainment shall we choose to do? How can

a society draw out members' talents and weave them into a polished performance which will capture the interest of an audience and make them sit up and say 'What a marvellous show—how we've enjoyed it!'

The choice made will depend upon a number of circumstances such as the environment in which the club is situated, the tastes of its members, the facilities available and a dozen other considerations. Sophisticated town clubs may choose to stage a thought-provoking serious drama. A youth club will probably prefer to do a light-hearted revue, a church group might produce a play with a religious or moral message, and others may consider putting on a pantomime, a historical play in mime, an extravaganza of song, old time music hall, a dance drama, a 'happening' or even 'drag'. But the ingredients for producing any type of show and shaping it into a finished performance are much the same for all.

Making a start

Begin by announcing your intention of putting on a show and invite members to join in and help. Stress the fact that you want not only actors, but people who can sew, paint, write, play music or who have knowledge of business matters and other talents. Call a meeting to discuss the project and appoint a chairman, secretary and treasurer. From this nucleus of people a committee can be formed and further officers appointed when necessary.

Collect some money at this early stage by running a coffee morning, jumble or 'bring and buy' sale which should raise enough to buy essential items such as music, make-up, material for costumes and the occasional props.

Producing a play

There are so many types of dramatic performance and the subject has such ramifications that the best plan is for those contemplating this type of entertainment to visit the public library and carefully study one of the many excellent books on producing a play. *Problems of Acting and Play Production* by Edwin C. White (Pitman) provides detailed advice for the novice. It is also advisable to seek the services of a drama teacher through contacting local colleges of further education or the County Drama Adviser. He or she will be an enormous help especially with a first production. In this way, pitfalls can be avoided and the quality of the performance can grow out of this.

Old time music hall

Get hold of some sheet music of old songs, ballads and sketches which can be obtained from Keith Prowse (address page 124). Watch the *Good Old Days* on television for more ideas for short sketches and melodrama. Include some community singing of popular favourites during the programme.

This type of entertainment benefits considerably if seating can be arranged around small tables. If the event is being held to raise money, blocks of tickets can be sold which book a table and in the interval, slices of pork pie, and pickled onions, beer, cider and coffee can be provided.

Whatever type of show is being produced, costumes are very important and especially for old time music hall. Help and information can be gleaned by looking in illustrated books in the library. Colleges of art can be consulted for advice on details and possible further assistance. Costumes can often be borrowed from other dramatic societies and schools in the area for a small sum, or hired from a professional firm such as Homburgs Theatrical Agency (address page 123).

Many amateur groups thoroughly enjoy making or adapting their own clothes. This is very satisfying to those who love to create and it is surprising what can be found in attics and wardrobes. Sheets, curtains, tablecloths and all manner of unlikely pieces of material can be turned into effective costumes with trimmings, dyes and imagination. *Stage Costumes and How to Make Them* by Julia Thompson (Pitman) gives simple instructions.

The mime

Much pleasure is derived from miming or improvising situations. Sometimes a number of groups are given a title which they portray in their individual way. Attitudes to topical questions can be played out, or Greek mythology, fairy stories, legends, ballads, folk tales acted with or without the aid of words. Imaginary scenery and props can be introduced and appropriate music played on the gramophone or piano.

When members become more confident, they might like to try performing plays in mime, depicting the history of their own district. Local historians are sometimes willing to suggest a list of important events, legends and traditions which have taken place in the past and from this suitable incidents can be selected.

The play can be performed with or without a narrator. If the latter, the characters must learn to synchronize movements with the words. There is an excellent book called *Teaching Mime* by Rose Bruford (Methuen) which gives instruction in the technique of this subject as well as a selection of suitable plays to perform.

A pageant

This is a more ambitious project but it is probably one of the most satisfying types of performance to produce. Many amateur societies can and do put on a pageant and anybody contemplating such an exciting project should first contact local historians and try to get hold of a copy of the book *Pageants* by Anthony Parker (The Bodley Head). This is now out of print but may be obtained through the library service who will also usually provide invaluable help to producers with the study of costumes, customs, scenery and effects. Local castles or ancient buildings which have links with the past make ideal settings for this type of performance.

In Scotland, a Pageant of the Nations was staged by eighteen Townswomen's Guilds. A narrator gave a description of the costumes, history and customs of each country as members paraded. The National Association of Women's Clubs produced a pageant of 'The Story of Bristol' with words and songs woven into a story taken from past events. Often such productions are backed up by displays of models of castles and battle scenes, coats of arms and dolls in costumes.

Music and song

Making music enhances any social occasion and clubs of all shapes and sizes give immense pleasure to others in this way. Help is often available from County Music Advisers, and those considering getting up a choral or orchestral performance of any size would do well to enquire at their Local Education Authority to see what help and advice can be offered.

The scope of amateur music making in this country is overwhelming. Performances given range from a small choir singing simple carols, a cantata or madrigals, to a large one presenting a complete opera. A most notable example is that of 'The Brilliant and the Dark', an operatic sequence for women's voices put on by The Women's Institutes at the Albert Hall in 1969.

Sometimes a programme of music and song may have a literary or historical theme running through it which helps with continuity and gives shape to the production. A women's society in Northamptonshire performed a programme called 'Folk Songs Round the World' with artists dressed in the national costume of each country.

Dancing

This form of entertainment is not restricted to the female sex by any means. All through the centuries, morris dancers and sword dancers have displayed their talents, and they still draw large audiences. Club members, regardless of sex and interested in getting up an entertainment of dancing should contact The English Folk Dance and Song Society (address page 122). Teachers are available to help and advise on public performances of this nature in all parts of Britain (see page 52).

The National Association of Women's Clubs in Surrey staged a Dance Drama with the theme of 'China' (the pottery, not the country). The first scene consisted of classic Greek dancers dressed in white robes depicting 'Wedgwood' against a background of blue curtains. A Dutch clog dance followed to represent Delft china, then a minuet before a beautiful Royal Doulton tableau. The haunting story of the Willow Pattern plate was enacted as a moving finale.

Film shows

Literally hundreds of films are available. These can be hired through various distributors and obtained on free loan or for a small fee. Many firms, travel agencies, embassies and educational organizations will also loan films free, including some firms who are no longer able to supply demonstrators because of the need to economize.

The subjects of these films are classified into the following headings:—

> Documentary
> Entertainment
> Industrial
> Religious
> Educational
> Medical
> General

To give a few examples, *British Transport Films* provide films on the activities of British Rail, London Transport, the British Road Services and a number of holiday and natural history films. *Concord Film Council* offers films on various charities and many on special human problems that lead to discussion. The *ICI Film Library* supplies films on refrigeration, terylene and weeding the garden. *The Gas Council* offers a series of films on cookery, conversion to North Sea gas and other subjects. See the Appendix for a list of addresses where catalogues and further information can be obtained.

Decide first what subject you would like to learn about. Then consult the catalogues to find out where to hire the film required. Can you afford a fee or must the film be free? How long running time is allowed? Is it to be followed by a discussion? The following equipment will be necessary:—

A large screen.

Table for projector.

16 mm sound projector or amplifier (usually available for hire from the County Education Authority or perhaps through the Local Education Department).

The hall or room where the film is to be shown must be adequately blacked out.

Ideally the operator should be experienced in handling this equipment, but novices should ask to have some instruction in using the machine before borrowing to ensure success.

It is usual for the client to pay return postage and a certificate of posting must be obtained to cover the hirer from loss in the post. All films are sent out in good order and in case of accident do not repair but report damage to supplier.

Mannequin parades

Often local dress shops and boutiques are willing to stage a professional show. The shop benefits through the publicity it receives and the audience gets a free and attractive entertainment as well as practical ideas for improving their own wardrobes.

Members sometimes make their own clothes and parade in them too which makes the whole thing more interesting. Others take a theme such as 'One Hundred Years of Fashion' or 'Fashion Through the Ages' and borrow, beg or make the styles themselves.

Pantomimes

These are a regular feature of many a club Christmas party or social. Any well known title can be built up into an entertaining burlesque with the addition of topical songs and sketches. Pantomime has fairly rigid conventions though. A principal 'boy', a pretty principal girl, a 'dame' who is a cosy caricature of womanhood, a wicked demon and a fairy godmother are all essential. But apart from these characters and the basic plot, there is plenty of room for ingenuity when writing the script by using local situations and settings. There should be a ballet—for both male and female dancers if possible—and time for the audience to join in with a catchy song. And the whole show should be just a bit larger than life.

At our society's Christmas party, members put on a potted pantomime of Snow White. The seven dwarfs were rather on the heavy side and when they sat down together on a long form, the whole thing splintered, sending them sprawling on the floor! Of course, this brought the house down and lifted the show into a never-to-be-forgotten category of its own.

The variety show

Under this heading comes the cabaret, revue, concert party, Black and White Minstrel show and others in similar vein.

Putting on an entertainment of this nature is often easier than producing a play because less corporate rehearsing is required and the work is more evenly distributed among the cast. This sort of show must be swinging and snappy with a lively pianist and a compère with plenty of jokes up his sleeve.

After a bright and breezy opening chorus, the comic turns should be separated by the couple who dance or the straight singer or instrumentalist. Introduce a sketch here and there and save the star turn until last. No item should last more than seven minutes, and preferably less.

The programme should be well balanced and this means taking care not to invite two artists with the same talents. A producer I know made this fatal mistake once and the rivalry between the two sopranos caused such friction that in the end he called the whole show off!

Occasionally a club or society is lucky and among its members is a person—perhaps an eccentric—who is an absolute natural on stage. I know somebody who convulses the audience even when making a perfectly straight announcement. Producers should always be on the look-out for a member who may have this priceless gift and make full use of it, especially in a show of this nature.

Copyright
Unfortunately, there are several laws governing entertainments. Any dramatic performance given in public by a society must pay acting fees. Copyright exists for the period of an author's life and for fifty years after his death. Permission must be obtained from the playwright or his agent to perform any play. This applies to musical copyright also and includes the playing of gramophone records. Permission must be granted by The Performing Right Society and The Phonographic Performance Ltd (addresses page 124).

Chapter 6

Raising funds

Most clubs need to raise money for something. It may be to pay off their own debts in order to survive at all. Or perhaps money is needed for a special project, such as to buy copies of music for the choir concert, a large urn for making tea or even for major structural alterations to the headquarters itself. Often clubs like to entertain old people or handicapped children and take them on an outing, or support other worthy schemes going on in their town, village or suburb. And there are also the national charities to which many societies contribute regular donations.

How to organize a function
Let the committee or a specially appointed committee plan the event.
1 Decide:—
    (a) how much you are aiming for,
    (b) if it is to be done in one event or a series of efforts,
    (c) the date, time and place of the first event,
    (d) the time limit for the whole project.
2 Decide on the nature of the function. If it is intended to attract large crowds, think big and check that:—
    (a) the date is clear in the Town Diary preventing a clash with other local functions. (See also page 56).
    (b) the type of entertainment or the particular celebrities you want are available on the chosen date.
    (c) the place you are holding it is available.
3 Decide who is to carry it through.
    (a) Are just your own members helping?

    (b) Are other organizations to be asked to help?

    (c) If it's a town affair, split the effort into sections and arrange sub-committees with responsibility for a section.

    (d) If it's a very small effort, individuals have to be asked personally.

4 Having booked the date:—

    (a) Notify all strategic sources, promising details later.

    (b) When plans are sufficiently advanced, issue a press release (see page 104) to all editors of newspapers within a twenty mile radius of base. Try to include some aspect of the entertainment which is unusual and will entice the public to come. It might be a visiting personality, a special sideshow for the children, an exceptional catering effort or some particularly good bargains.

    (c) If the function warrants it, sell programmes as publicity and as tickets.

    (d) Arrange for posters, press advertisements and publicity notes to be sent to secretaries of other organizations (and perhaps car stickers and road banners).

    (e) Write personal letters to local firms, large shops and factories asking for their support, a donation or a prize for a raffle. Many large organizations run house magazines and would probably be willing to include an announcement of the function if requested.

What type of function?

Much depends upon the environment of a society when considering what type of fund raising event to hold. Look with a calculating eye and consider what your area has to offer which might be put to use as a potential money raiser. For instance, at a spectacular country garden near my home which is open to the public throughout the summer, a coffee stall is manned by volunteers each Sunday with profits going to a local charity. A Women's Institute traced the owner of a disused water mill in their seaside village, and he gave them permission to open it as a temporary gift shop containing goods donated by a number of other Institutes. And in Preston, £1,209 was raised by a Ladies Circle which held a mammoth 'Good as New' three-day sale held in an empty supermarket. Vacant shops can often be turned into money raisers for all kinds of sales as well as using the windows for promoting forthcoming events and displaying prizes and raffles.

During a jazz festival on the Isle of Wight, Round Tablers and their wives raised £1,400 serving refreshments to 5,000 hairy youngsters. At one traffic 'bottleneck' outside Romsey in Hampshire, Scouts serve hot dogs by the road side every Sunday, providing a service very profitably. Learn to seize any opportunity which may present itself and don't be afraid to ask those in authority to lend you practical assistance. All sorts of unlikely buildings and activities may turn out to be gold mines. But check carefully with local police to be certain to avoid breaking regulations.

Celebrities

A local celebrity may be willing to be a guest of honour at a luncheon, to open a fete or bazaar, knock down piles of pennies, run in a pancake race, judge carnivals, give away prizes at a ceremony, or play in a charity cricket match. Some celebrities are under obligation to their agents or managers and may not undertake these functions without charging a heavy fee. Unless they are exceedingly well known and likely to draw huge crowds the outlay is not worth the return. And if large crowds did come, could you cope with them? Consider this point carefully and make provision for sufficient refreshments, car parking and cloakrooms.

Individual efforts

The members of your club can be encouraged to exploit their talents in order to raise cash. In a town famous for its football team, youth club members knit bobble caps and scarves in supporters' colours. A friend of mine bakes Christmas puddings in November and sells to friends and neighbours. Perhaps members could join together to pick fruit in local farms and orchards. Issuing each member with say 50p and asking them to trade with it can reap some amazing results. And market stalls are very cheap to hire and are extremely good money spinners. Apply to the market superintendent at your local Council Offices for permission, planning well in advance. There are all sorts of other individual ways in which people can make money and although the financial gain may seem small, it mounts up when the efforts are regular over a period of time.

On the following pages I have described some of the more unusual forms of fund raising rather than the run-of-the-mill jumble sales, coffee mornings and so on. These suggestions will not be new to everybody, but all have been run successfully in the recent past, and I hope they will give fresh inspiration to fund raisers.

A hostess society entertains

Vast sums of money have been raised by an enterprising society which, on a number of occasions, has entertained other clubs and associations drawn from outlying towns and villages. This host society meets visitors as they arrive by coach at a well known rose garden situated just outside the town. Here, the visitors enjoy the magnificent displays of colourful flowerbeds and in the church hall are afterwards entertained to tea or supper, provided by members of the catering committee.

Where do the visiting parties come from? During the preceding winter, the organizer draws a circle of, say, a

50-mile radius. Letters are sent to all clerks of Town Halls, Council Offices and Parish Councils in these areas asking for addresses of recreational societies and coach operators in their districts. From each list of societies, the organizer sorts out those most likely to be attracted to an outing of this nature. Back goes a letter, offering the selected society an invitation with details of the proposed events, with times and the inclusive price. Coach operators are interested because they find it difficult to procure caterers willing to supply meals for coach parties, particularly if supper is required.

Of course, this means hard work for the catering committee, who must provide the teas or the cold meat and salad supper to large numbers of people with the speed of lightning.

'But we have no rose gardens,' you may plead. Maybe not, but what else has your district to offer? Negotiate with the owners of anything which is interesting or unusual, but if your search yields nothing, don't despair. A tour of the village, a visit to a member's pretty garden, a simple walk along the towpath of the river can all be substituted for the more elaborate programme. It is the personal and friendly aspect of this outing which really counts, the introduction of one club to another, the exchange of ideas and the bait of a home-made tea or supper which makes the event an attraction.

An art show with a special theme

Does your town boast a picturesque church, castle, monument, ancient house, street scene or a beauty spot of special interest to artists and photographers? Then why not mount an art exhibition extolling its beauty, preferably during a weekend or over a Bank Holiday period?

Begin by writing to art and photographic societies in your area asking if members would be prepared to lend any artistic efforts depicting the subject you wish to exhibit.

If an artist is willing to sell a picture an arrangement can be made whereby a percentage of the sale figure is retained.

The local newspaper office may have a store of photographs and be willing to lend these too. Preservation societies which exist for the care and maintenance of old properties often have pictorial records of buildings and street scenes which would add much interest to such a project.

Art schools and Colleges of Adult Education offer further hunting grounds in which organizers can seek material, not only in the field of painting, but embroidered collages of the subject are sometimes executed in the needlework and embroidery departments.

Charge an entrance fee for the exhibition or ask for a donation if this is preferred. Extra profits can be made by serving refreshments, running a cake stall and inviting viewers to place coppers beside their favourite choice in each section.

Individual exhibitions
Small exhibitions of all kinds provide excellent sources of cash for fund raisers and can easily be mounted in a member's own home and sometimes in a room at the library. Whether the collection consists of dolls, pipes, china, silver or anything else, the public are often willing to give a donation to a cause for the privilege of seeing it. A friend of mine raised the incredible sum of £60 this way by collecting together tapestries made by talented people living in the district and displaying them in her large sitting room. This exhibition was open for several days and a raffle, bring and buy, and cake stall helped to bump up profits. Of course, a lot of hard work had been put into the project by the organizer beforehand, who delivered dozens of individual postcards all round the neighbourhood inviting people to come and see the exhibition.

A flower collection and sale

Many garden lovers grow more flowers than they need at certain times of the year (particularly from mid-July to mid-August, and from mid-September to mid-October) and are willing to give them away to help a good cause. Ask friends and neighbours if they will co-operate and arrange to collect and distribute as follows.

Contact large firms, factories and petrol stations in the area asking if they would agree to the erection of a sales table in the car park of their premises at the time employees leave work on Friday evenings. The tables should be manned if possible and bear large notices giving the name of the cause, the price of each bunch of flowers (placed in buckets of water) and a strong collection box with a slot for the money to be inserted if a seller is not able to be there. Naturally the price should be kept low and 10p has been found to be a satisfactory figure.

Money from recipes

New ideas for presenting food never fail to arouse interest. But the public needs to be enticed to sample them in a novel way.

Producing a recipe book

A group of N.S.P.C.C. helpers in a market town raised a considerable amount of money and gave pleasure to supporters and friends by putting the following idea into practice.

A notice in the library, letters to editors of local newspapers and women's organizations in the district invited members of the public to send their favourite recipes for proposed inclusion in a cookery book. Duplicated forms were provided so that various facts could be recorded and collated by the editors. These were assembled into appropriate chapters and finally sent to the printers. Meanwhile, tradesmen in the district were asked to buy advertising space and in fact, this money covered the cost of printing 1,000 copies of the book which sold at 37½p each.

A launching party to promote its sale was laid on at the Town Hall. All the contributors were notified of the event and as they felt they had a personal stake in the book, practically all bought a copy and tickets for the party. An excellent meal was included in the price and the menu was selected from the contents of the book and cooked by the organizers. The event attracted publicity and promoted further sales.

Taste and Try

Keen cooks might like to run a food tasting evening which seems to provide a lot of satisfaction to the participants as well as making a profit. Each member makes her favourite dish and brings it to the meeting and sells a helping for 2p. If guests want a copy of the recipe as well they must pay double. It is surprising how the money mounts up.

A sponsored swim or 'sausage and splash'

Everybody knows about the sponsored walk, but how about the sponsored swim? Contact the local swimming pool and see if it is possible to hire the pool for an evening in mid-summer. Invite members and also the public to enter for the contest and to collect as many sponsors as they can to back them per length. Provide duplicated forms for competitors to collect sponsors' signatures and the amount they are willing to pay.

Meanwhile, see if the Scouts, Guides or any other local youth group can be persuaded to run a barbecue providing hot dogs and coffee to keep supporters and contestants warm and energetic. Hire a marquee if the grounds are large enough and install a band for dancing after the contest is over.

Running a barbecue in this way on a borrowed field is an easy and satisfactory method of raising funds even without the sponsored swim first.

A food and wine festival

Food and drink are subjects close to the heart of every man and woman in the world. So why not run a special festival to encourage the public to indulge in these pleasures?

Contact every food and wine shop in the area and offer free publicity and display space providing they are willing to give away samples of their wares to the public. No sales whatsoever are permitted.

It sounds too simple to be true, doesn't it? But it really works, especially in well populated areas. The Lions Clubs in Southampton and district have raised vast sums of money over a period of time by charging the public 50p per head to spend an evening at one of these events. The only cost to the organizers is for the publicity and the hire of the hall.

Extra publicity can be obtained by issuing the retailers who will be exhibiting with raffle tickets which they can give to each customer in their shop who spends more than a given amount. These raffle tickets can only be placed in the drum in the exhibition hall after the customer has gained admission by buying an entrance ticket.

For large functions, other ways of increasing ticket sales are by presenting a bright cabaret spot, a beauty queen contest or an amateur talent competition. A publicity campaign can often be run in conjunction with the local newspapers in order to attract sufficient numbers of entries.

An ideal home and family exhibition

This festival idea can also take the form of an Ideal Home and Family Exhibition. Local shops concerned with the sale of merchandise for homes can be approached and offered a stall and for this type of event, shop owners are usually willing to pay for the privilege so that the public need not pay for entrance. The advantage to the public is that they can ask unlimited questions without obligation and see all the merchandise under one roof.

Contacts can include shops and firms dealing with deep freezers, house insulation, lighting, upholstery, hi-fi, gardening and all kinds of hobby interests. Special demonstrations can be arranged with the assistance of the Gas and Electricity Boards, beauty counsellors, wig fitters, sewing machine and cake icing experts. Film shows, mannequin parades, gift and cake stalls, 'good as new' clothing sales and other tried and tested money raising methods can be thrown in for good measure.

Chapter 7

Self-help and social service

Friendship through service to each other and to the community is the motto adopted by many clubs in this country. And surely there is no more admirable and public-spirited aim or object. Nevertheless, it is not always so simple and straightforward to help others as might be supposed. Members may have a burning desire to put the whole world right, starting with each other, but those they wish to help would often rather struggle on alone with their problems. To illustrate this point, my own father at the age of ninety-one, was incensed to find that his next door neighbour had come round and kindly shovelled the snow away from the front path. The following morning, to make sure this did not happen again, he set his alarm for 7 a.m. and went out to do it himself!

However, it is surprising how often members of a club have the same sort of difficulties and are only too happy to offer each other practical assistance once they know they need it. So let us look first within the society and begin by learning to help ourselves and each other. Then, when this has been achieved, we can look outwards to the community in which we live and find out where voluntary service is most needed.

Helping ourselves and each other

The first step is for somebody to be appointed a social service secretary to get a plan working. He or she can draw up a duplicated list of proposed services which it is hoped to provide and members can be asked to tick those items which appeal. For instance, in a club where membership consists entirely of women it might look something like this:—

Are you interested in taking part in any of the following schemes by helping to form:—

A baby sitting rota.

A pre-school play-group or a weekly crèche.

A car pool for taking and fetching children to and from school.

A 'helping hands' scheme for members' families faced with a domestic crisis.

Or arranging:—

Transport to enable members to shop, get to meetings, church, etc.

Visits to members in hospital or at home and perhaps taking tape recordings of meetings for them to hear.

Delivery of cards, presents or flowers to members on appropriate occasions.

Once the social service secretary has the names of members interested in any of the schemes, she has something on which to work. It doesn't matter whether they want to give or receive help. The important thing is to arrange friendly meetings between members who wish to be involved in any one project, so that the ideas can be put into action and a leader appointed for each section.

Other ways in which members of a society can help each other are as follows.

A sales table

This offers financial advantage to members. At each meeting, unwanted items can change hands at profit to the owner with a small percentage retained by the club. All kinds of surplus garden and market produce finds willing buyers as well as handicrafts, jams and pickles, cakes, good-as-new clothes, unwanted gifts and anything else which is in good condition. But make it clear that articles which come into the category of junk or jumble cannot be accepted.

Bulk buying scheme
General household supplies such as electric light bulbs, paper tissues, toilet soap, instant coffee and many other essential household commodities can be bought at a much reduced overall figure from such firms as John Dron Ltd (address page 121). The items bought cheaply in bulk can then be distributed individually amongst members, but organizers should take the names of those wishing to buy before ordering, to find out if the demand is sufficient.

A library
Members are often willing to give books which are of special interest to others in the club. These can form the basis of a small, but valuable library. Club funds, when particularly healthy, can be used to purchase new books if members are in agreement.

These ideas and many more can be adapted with success in any type of club and varied according to its needs. The vital thing is for organizers to discover what members want and provide it by asking the others for help and co-operation.

Demand and supply will fluctuate and organizers must keep a watchful eye and ear on all the schemes and step in with fresh ideas, suggestions, and adaptations as the needs arise.

Helping in the community
We in Britain may well be living in a welfare state, but there are many gaps in the social services waiting to be filled by people who can be relied upon to turn up when a promise to do so has been given. Of course, they need to be concerned and to care for others too, as well as having time and energy to spare.

Discovering who needs help

Sometimes, offers of voluntary service in an area are so generous that there is serious overlapping of good works. Two or three clubs may be visiting and taking out numbers of old people, while the unmarried mothers remain isolated and desperately lonely in their bedsitters. At the orphanage there may be a waiting list of prospective 'aunties', while down the next road new immigrants flounder helplessly with a new language, different foods, strange schools for their children and insurmountable housing problems. If we are genuinely sincere in our desire to help those in need, we should be willing to give where the need is greatest and to take the trouble to find out what kind of help is most required.

To make sure that the efforts of volunteers are directed into the best possible channels and that no section of the community's needs are overlooked, organizers should set about co-ordinating voluntary work with others in the district. Contact the Council of Social Service, a social worker or the Citizen's Advice Bureau if the club is situated in a town. If it exists in a remote country area, arrangements should be made to meet the vicar, doctor, district nurse, welfare officer or parish councillors to discuss when and where help is most needed.

Lonely people of all ages, but particularly the old, can often be discovered by discreet questioning of tradespeople and others who know the district intimately. Often these people would not ask those in authority to help, but would probably appreciate a friendly visit from an individual.

Sometimes there are announcements in the local paper asking for help in a crisis. Last winter, a number of the staff at our local Old People's Home were struck down with 'flu' and Matron wrote a letter to the newspaper asking for voluntary, temporary help. Members of the Ladies Circle answered the call and moved in to assist with bed making, feeding patients, washing false teeth and tackling other unsavoury tasks with cheerful fortitude.

Organizing volunteers

The first and most important job for the social service secretary is to collect the names of those members willing to help in some way but never mind in which direction at this stage. The next task is to find out where help is required from the authorities and match the jobs to the volunteers. The best method is as follows:—

1 Make a map of the area, subdividing it into convenient districts.
2 Make a list of the jobs to be done and have copies duplicated and distributed widely.
3 Invite all members and friends to volunteer and attend a special meeting.
4 Allocate volunteers to the districts in which they live if possible, and select a leader for each section.
5 Call together the leaders and discuss the work and methods of tackling it in more detail.
6 Leaders will then call together their own groups and allocate the work in the best possible way with the helpers available.
7 When the scheme is well under way, get somebody with a talent to produce an attractive leaflet which can be printed or duplicated. This can describe the work being done by members and may well encourage others to join.

Soon after the schemes are launched, and from time to time, it is advisable for the leaders to get together to discuss how the programmes are working out. Ideas can be pooled and much learnt from the successes and failures of others. I know how I felt when first visiting a geriatric ward of twenty-four patients of whom a large number were deaf. Only after discussion with those more experienced did I learn to bend down close to the patient's ear, to raise my voice sufficiently and to ask THEM questions. They long to talk to somebody about the times when they were young and of their homes and families and not about what is happening now. When members share these actual experiences they become better equipped to overcome their feelings of helplessness when confronted with similar situations.

Apart from helping in old people's homes, what other kinds of voluntary help are welcome? Naturally this depends on where members live, but here are some ideas which social service secretaries can investigate to see if help is needed in their particular districts.

Home visiting

This service is mainly directed towards the housebound, whether lonely, old, blind or handicapped in any way. Visits can take the form of a friendly chat, reading or writing letters, bringing in shopping and generally being useful where necessary. Teaching a craft is greatly appreciated too and can make all the difference to the well-being of a housebound person. Men who can mend fuses, do simple carpentry, garden, decorate rooms and clean outhouses are always in demand. Sitting in with old people or invalids to relieve relatives and attendants who would like an afternoon or evening out occasionally, is another worthwhile service.

Home visiting can be extended to include those people just discharged from hospitals, mental and other institutions, and further information can be obtained from local Old People's Welfare Committees, Councils of Social Service and the W.R.V.S.

Meals on wheels

This service is run by the W.R.V.S. who are almost always grateful for volunteers with or without cars. It entails delivering hot midday meals to elderly, sick or housebound people who are not able to shop or cook adequately for themselves. Through taking part in this service, voluntary workers can see how best they might help old people in other ways. Some clubs undertake to cook and deliver a meals on wheels breakfast on Christmas morning.

Visiting and helping in hospitals and institutions

Helpers are often welcome to visit and talk to long-stay patients and perhaps take them for walks, to assist with serving meals and feeding patients. Unskilled nursing help is also required with blanket bathing, making beds and other simple tasks.

Members with special skills such as hairdressing, beauty culture and handicrafts can be utilized to help cheer patients up and get them interested in life again. Assistance is often needed, too, with running a library or shopping trolley, typing or addressing envelopes, sewing or mending garments, flower arranging, running messages or escorting patients from one department to another. And sometimes maternity hospitals are grateful for voluntary workers to sit in with patients in labour when they might otherwise be left on their own.

In this category, mention should be made of opportunities which may exist in towns to help in health centres, in baby and child welfare, family planning, blood donation and other special clinics. Day centres for old people and the handicapped are springing up everywhere and help is often welcome with catering, reception work, filing of notes or filling in forms. Further information can be obtained through contacting the local Public Health Department.

Hospital broadcasting service

This is an up-and-coming service run by voluntary workers in their spare time. The job entails going round the wards, talking to patients and asking them for record requests. These and items of local interest and news form most of the programme content, but local personalities are often interviewed in between the record playing. Sometimes tape recorded talks with patients are put out as well. Record requests played for patients in the children's wards are particularly appreciated. Enquire at local hospitals to see if a service is operated and if help is required.

The hospital car service
Volunteers are always needed to transport patients to and from their homes to hospital and to treatment clinics and on other journeys. Car owners who would like to help in this way can claim a mileage allowance. Drivers are required to take house- and institution-bound patients for a drive, to church, or to other events.

There is new group of people called 'Contact' living within an hour's drive of central London. This movement began when members of a club (six drivers and six helpers) arranged monthly Sunday drives in private cars for twelve old people at a time. Now there are several more groups, always of the same size. The old people, who often live alone in poor conditions, enjoy the gardens and the friendly atmosphere of a home. They are able to meet others in the same circumstances who come in different cars, and they benefit by having a regular event of this nature to look forward to. This activity might well be copied by clubs in country districts who live within striking distance of a large town where names of suitable passengers can be obtained from the Old People's Welfare Committee.

Helping in other clubs
Many opportunities exist for giving help to clubs for the mentally and physically handicapped, the hard of hearing, for old people and especially the new immigrants. Time to

visit and talk to members is deeply appreciated. Any skills are welcome such as the ability to organize folk dancing, keep fit, games and sports, a sing-song or to teach first aid. Those who can play the piano or entertain in any way, be it conjuring, showing transparencies of holidays, blowing the bugle or anything else, are much in demand. Lists of societies which exist in a town can be found at public libraries and offers to help can be made direct.

A number of towns have started up special immigrant associations. Volunteers are needed to give lessons in English as well as to talk and help bewildered immigrants in any way they can. Letters can be sent to schools, colleges and factories asking for names and addresses of foreign students and workers. Then friendly invitations can be sent to attend a special meeting or social.

Hospitality in the home
New residents, unmarried mothers, foreigners and those living away from their own homes all appreciate being entertained, especially at weekends when they are likely to be extra lonely. Old people, too, love to be invited out to tea with a family. The Council of Social Service and Old People's Welfare Committees would put members in touch with lonely people.

Voluntary work with children
Opportunities for helping in crèches, playgroups, nursery schools, baby clinics, child welfare clinics, orphanages, children's homes, hospitals and institutions exist in many towns. Men and women with experience are also needed to become uncles and aunties to orphans, or to foster children for short or long stay periods, and if living in the country, to give a holiday to a town child. Sometimes when a mother is ill or has to go into hospital, motherly help is needed to look after the children. Local Children's Departments will

supply further information on where voluntary help of this nature is required.

Here are some slightly more unusual ways in which members might like to help children.

Making tea or coffee in a youth club (offer direct help). Teaching young children road safety. Contact the Tufty Clubs National Organizer (address page 124). Giving after-care hospitality to a Borstal boy or girl from a remand home (contact local Children's Department). Forming a 'link' group to visit wards of mentally handicapped children. Members play, talk and take an interest in the small patients. Contact mental hospitals or Public Health Department.

Campaigning for local causes

Are any of your members deeply concerned about the way in which their town, suburb or village is run? Do they feel strongly about its local council, public services, town planning, housing problems, road safety, juvenile delinquency, the lack of nursery schools, care of the aged, or anything else? Any one person can canvass for reform or improvements if they feel strongly enough, but if they have the support of their society, this will strengthen their claim considerably.

The reformer must then set to work to influence others too. This means writing letters to newspapers, councillors, MPs and other influential people and associations. Reports must be submitted to appropriate bodies and public speeches made to anybody who is willing to listen.

Clubs can tackle almost anything if there is sufficient enthusiasm. Some raise money to buy large old houses with the help of local councils to convert into flats for old people or unmarried mothers. Other run mammoth anti-litter campaigns, or nag medical officers of health and others in authority to provide family planning clinics, to put fluoride in the water or take it out, to provide help for drug addicts, or a day centre for the handicapped. But whatever needs doing in your community will stand a better chance of being put right by canvassing for public support through the medium of your society.

Voluntary help is of inestimable value in any community, but it's no good expecting to succeed in every effort. Don't be discouraged when things go wrong. It is amazing what perseverance will achieve. Be cheerful, look attractive, don't be patronizing in your attitude and genuinely care about the people you are trying to help. Never expect to be thanked and remember that their pleasure is your reward for whatever is done in the sweet name of charity.

Chapter 8

Attracting new members and publicizing your society

Do you want your club to thrive and be successful? Of course you do. But if this is to happen, it must constantly look outside itself to attract new members who will pour fresh vitality, ideas and energy into it. A club whose membership remains static becomes dull and inward looking and the whole thing may grind to a halt however hard the committee works for its success.

There are many ways in which the public can be alerted to the existence of a society. The most simple is by just telling other people, whether by word, letter or public speaking. Then there is the valuable medium of the press, radio and possibly television in the future. And finally, there is much publicity to be gained by the mounting of special exhibitions, projects and shows, illustrating the activities, aims and objects of a particular organization (see Chapter 4). All these methods will help to promote the society and bring increased membership at the same time.

The press officer

Begin by appointing a press officer who has plenty of bounce and is friendly, communicative and persevering. His or her job is to report activities of the club and to capture the interest of the public. If people don't know about a club and what it does, how can they possibly be inspired to join?

Let us begin by exploring the most simple methods of promoting a society.

The personal approach

Members can be asked to make personal calls on people in

the neighbourhood, particularly new residents who might be interested to visit the club as a guest one evening. Visitors who accept the invitation should be escorted, looked after throughout the meeting and introduced to other members and guests. Offering personal attention makes all the difference to a shy person who needs special encouragement to overcome the hurdle of walking into a room full of people, let alone becoming a member of a society.

Mailing schemes
Personal letters (or duplicated if volunteer writers are short) can be sent to all those people in a district whom it is thought might be interested in the activities of a club (see page 111 for example letter). This can be followed up with another letter giving more details, together with an enclosed postcard to be returned if the recipient is not interested. If this is not sent back, a personal visit can be made to the house inviting them along.

A special guest night
This is one of the most effective methods of attracting new members. Each member invites a friend, relative or neighbour to a special meeting where refreshments, a good speaker and some form of entertainment is offered free of charge. Money should be raised within the club beforehand (see Chapter 6) in order to defray costs.

Posters (see page 112)
Much publicity can be gained for a society by placing posters of a semi-permanent nature in strategic positions, for instance, on the public library notice board, the Town Hall, in factories or whatever is the source for gaining members. Advertising in the personal columns of local newspapers also brings forth results.

Local newspapers

I am surprised, sometimes, to hear organizers refuse the offer of publicity in a newspaper. 'What purpose could a write-up serve?' they ask. Little do they realize the power of the printed word. Not only does it bring a society's existence to the notice of the general public, but it alerts the attention of the authorities and other important local institutions in the area. This pays handsomely when a club is programme planning and in need of speakers, demonstrators and invitations to places of interest.

Many editors are willing to give a regular 'spot' to the activities of a local society. Write, asking to be included giving full particulars of the society's aims and objects and main activities. Reports are preferred typed, but if this is not possible, maximum spacing should be used and names and other key words should be written in capitals. Use one side of quarto paper only and leave wide margins and put the name, address and telephone number of the press officer on any copy submitted.

Learn to make the most of this valuable free publicity. Be reliable in delivering reports by the deadline date and check on facts, spellings and grammatical errors. Give full weight to the most important activities such as the visit of the talented demonstrator, your latest achievements in the field of fund raising, news of your service for the housebound and similar items. Give names of members who deserve recognition because this helps to sell the newspaper, but leave out who won the raffle for the necklace made from liquorice allsorts and get the priorities in the right order.

To illustrate these points, there is the incredible story of an association who wrote a report of their meeting and sent it in to the local newspaper as follows: 'The chairman opened the meeting and introduced the speaker. The prize for the greatest number of articles beginning with the letter B collected in a jam jar went to Mrs Snelgrove. The raffle for a set of egg cosies was won by Mrs Blenkinsop. Mrs Orpington made the cakes and tea was served by Mrs Snodgrass. Plans were discussed to visit the youth club pantomime. Unfortunately, whilst playing "Follow My Leader", the chairman, Mrs Heckingbottom, had a heart attack and died.'

Further publicity can be gained in newspapers by sending in extra reports concerning special activities especially if accompanied by a photograph. If the newspaper cannot supply a photographer, arrange for an amateur to take one preferably two weeks before the event. Send this with the account of the forthcoming function and remember that photographs must have details on a separate sheet of paper giving names and initials of people in the photograph. Send complimentary tickets for the editor or a member of his staff to attend and delegate somebody knowledgeable to show them round and to introduce them to organizers and others concerned with the project. Build up further publicity by methods suggested in Chapter 9.

Local radio stations
Where local radio stations operate, clubs are indeed fortunate. At the time of going to press, there are eighteen established stations and plans are going ahead for more. This means that many parts of the country will have their own nerve centre with opportunities for clubs and societies to promote their aims, objects and activities.

How is contact gained with a local radio station? This is not easy because the skeleton staff is likely to be working under considerable pressure. A personal relationship should be established with the producer of the appropriate programme and the best way to achieve this is to telephone or call in at the station at regular intervals. Give only brief, bold headings at this stage, but be prepared to submit further information presented in a tight, factual and lively style. If this method of attack does not produce results, do what one society has done. Invite the producer to visit your club to tell you about the workings of the programme. This provides a good opportunity to fire questions and to find out how to open closed doors in the future.

Producing a news-sheet or magazine

What is the point of producing a news-sheet or magazine? In the first place, it generates goodwill both within and outside a society. It communicates ideas and provides a platform for the views and opinions of members as well as a factual record of activities. Above all, it arouses enthusiasm and, when distributed efficiently, encourages new members.

How do you go about it? First discuss the project with members and ask for contributions and help with the production of the magazine. A good typist, capable of making a stencil, is essential, and it is a great advantage if there is an artist among the members who can enliven the pages with the occasional sketch or diagram. Others can help with proof reading, lay-out, checking facts, correspondence and distribution. The use of a duplicator, preferably free of charge, is another essential, although later on, other forms of reproduction can be considered.

Financing the project is an important consideration and this might be overcome by charging a little for the finished product. Or perhaps the committee might be willing to allow a proportion of the subscriptions or a sum from club funds to go towards the cost. It may also be possible to sell space to local tradespeople, but this cannot be relied upon.

A news-sheet is a fairly simple undertaking, but a magazine can be tackled by the inexperienced too if there is sufficient enthusiasm and determination. To begin with, it can take the form of a simple four-fold, eight-page duplicated pamphlet, produced once or twice a year. If all goes well, the circulation can be increased to one issue a quarter or every month. The interest of readers is more easily sustained when issues arrive at short, regular intervals.

Most important of all, what sort of content should fill the pages? I have before me now a duplicated copy of a magazine produced by a group of women's clubs in an area. The cover bears their national emblem and an amusing cartoon of a blissful mother reading the magazine beneath a line of nappies. Inside there are ten pages containing the chairman's report, a piece about their recent rally and articles on activities both serious and gay. There are notes on results achieved through fund-raising efforts as well as amusing incidents and personal experiences. There are one or two poems, a description of the meal a member had produced for an old people's party, some questions and answers and announcements of forthcoming events.

Editors of club magazines are fortunate in that they will know many of the interests and hobbies, social backgrounds, academic ability, age and status of their readers. Begin by inviting members to write letters on any topic concerned with the club or about which they feel strongly. They are much more likely to contribute letters than articles to begin with, but from them ideas will germinate, controversial issues will develop and stories and articles will eventually emerge, providing encouragement is freely given. The various officers of the club can be asked to write the reports and whoever submits the best ones can be asked to take on the job of editing that section in the future.

Of course, it is not possible to cover every facet of producing a magazine in a book of this size. *Editing the Small Magazine* by Rowena Ferguson (Columbia University Press) is an excellent guide. Unfortunately it is out of print, but can sometimes be obtained through public libraries.

To sum up, an editor must work well in advance of his deadline and remember that a great deal of time must be spent in arranging page lay-outs and fitting in the material to the available space. Advice can often be sought from local journalists and by studying the finished work of others in the field, both amateur and professional. In time, he will get the 'hang' of how it's done and the result will be a successful magazine which will do nothing but good for the society and all who read it.

Chapter 9

Setting up a new society

Perhaps you have been inspired by reading this book and are thinking seriously of starting up a club of your own. And why not? It is surprisingly easy and those who have done it are full of pride and enthusiasm. So in this chapter I intend to give a simple step-by-step guide on how to start a society from scratch in your community.

Certainly there are hundreds of existing organizations which serve enthusiasts' needs very satisfactorily. Before setting up your own ramblers/photography/bee-keepers/ young wives or any other club, just make certain there is not a similar one flourishing in the next road. Call at the public library and scan the list of those already established in your area.

It may also be possible to form a branch of a parent society in your town. For instance, if arranging flowers fascinates you and your friends, contact The National Association of Flower Arrangement Societies. The same applies to Spastics, Spiders or the Veteran Car Club. Dozens of other special interests are catered for by organizations whose head-quarters may be in London or other large towns. Your library will find out if there is one serving your particular interest and supply you with the address. If you form a local branch of one of these societies, help, advice and information will be forthcoming from them and they will probably send an adviser down to the first meeting to get the club on its feet.

Once having satisfied yourself that nothing exists to fulfil your particular needs and that there is a genuine desire for a club of your type in the locality, go ahead and discuss it with your friends and those who share your hobby or interest. Then talk to those in authority in the district and see what they have to say.

Making a start

The other day I went along to a special inaugural meeting which had been arranged to launch a new society. I talked to the organizer and enthusiastic new members who happened to be young married women living on a nearby housing estate and I feel I cannot do better than describe exactly how this club got on its feet successfully. Although the information will apply specifically to starting a *women's club*, the broad principles for starting any type of society are much the same.

Begin by talking to those in authority in your district and in the case of a women's club this would be the social worker at the Town Hall or Council Offices. She knows the whole area and the problems of women, both married and single, better than you do. Listen to her advice which will be sound and based on a great deal of experience. Talk to others in authority, such as the local doctor, the librarian, play-group organizers, nursery and primary school headmistresses, and the nursing officer in charge of the maternity and welfare clinics. Tell them about the proposals, ask if they approve and if they would tell others and later on, display a poster on their premises.

A good time for getting any club going is the beginning of October or during the months of March to May. This means putting the following suggestions into action some weeks beforehand.

Write a letter to the editor of your local paper giving an account of your proposed society and ask him if he will print it. It could run something like this:—

The Editor,
The Southbridge Gazette,
Southbridge,
Northamptonshire.   4th September, 197—

Dear Sir,
  A number of wives on the Pedley Wood Estate have discussed the possibility of forming a women's club to serve the residents on the estate and surrounding areas. The main purpose of the meetings would be to get to know and help each other, as well as inviting speakers, organizing social events and holding interesting discussions. The club will be self-governing, non-political and non-sectarian.
  We hope to arrange an informal meeting to discuss the forming of such a club. Would anybody interested please ring Southbridge 4545?
                    Yours faithfully,
                                    Mary Linfield.

The preliminary meeting
When you have collected the names of a number of people who are definitely interested, call a meeting at your house. Make sure that each person knows the date, time and place where it is to be held. Write out roughly in advance what you are going to say and do. Prepare the room by placing the chairs in a circle and detail one of your friends to serve the coffee after the business has been discussed.
  At this first meeting, the important thing is to introduce everybody and to be friendly and informal. Make a special effort to remember everybody's name and where they live and get them all to write their names and addresses on a sheet of paper.
  Open the meeting (which should start promptly at the time stated) with a brief explanation of the aims and objects of the proposed club. Give an account of the type of activities

which you hope to provide and follow this up by throwing the meeting open to discussion. Encourage everybody to say what it is they hope such a society will offer and make a note of their suggestions. There may be somebody who wants to throw a spanner in the works, but don't let her put you off! Assuming that the majority of those present are in favour of the idea, elect a temporary committee for a period of three to six months. This 'caretaker' committee must undertake to arrange the early programmes and do other jobs as they arise. Once the club is on its feet, members can elect their own officers and committee on an annual basis and the caretaker committee can stand down.

Making a constitution

One of the first tasks will be to prepare for the inaugural public meeting at which the machinery will be set up for running the new society. A suggested constitution should be drawn up roughly as a working guide and worded as simply as possible. At this early stage the set-up must be fluid and flexible to allow for new ideas to be incorporated, but sufficiently organized to give stability and continuity. A draft constitution might be as follows:—

1 Aims of a group.
2 Membership (age range and who may join).
3 Subscription. This can be so much per year or so much per meeting.
4 Frequency of meetings—weekly, fortnightly or monthly, etc.
5 Officers required. Chairman, secretary, treasurer. A president also if there is somebody suitable for this office.
6 Membership of committee. (The committee can be elected later and should be in the ratio of one to every six to ten ordinary members).

7   Method of nominating chairman, officers and committee.

8   Length of time for holding office. It is wise to have a rule that officers and members of committee serve for three years and have to stand down for one year before being eligible for re-election. This ensures new blood and develops leadership.

9   Arrangements for annual general meeting.

Fixing the subscription

In order to finance the club, there must be an annual subscription unless it is decided to charge a fixed figure to be collected individually at each meeting. The amount will depend upon costs and the anticipated membership. It is advisable to keep the subscription as low as possible to begin with, so that hard-up potential members will not be discouraged from joining on this account. Nevertheless, it should be high enough to cover the hire of the hall, lighting and heating, speakers' fees, postage, telephone and incidental running expenses. Of course, the subscription will vary according to how much is paid for the hire of the hall. To take two examples, a flourishing women's society in our town charges its members only 15p a year subscription, plus 10p for each meeting which includes tea and biscuits. The subscription for our local Flower Arrangement Society is 75p per year which covers the cost of tea and biscuits too. Some clubs serve refreshments at cost, others set out to make a profit. Many help financial matters along by asking members to give a raffle prize from time to time, so that a healthy profit is made from the sale of tickets. Fund raising, through coffee mornings, jumble sales and bring and buy sales, etc., provides extra finance as required.

Where to hold the meetings

There is, of course, nothing to stop clubs meeting in a

member's own home or taking it in turn to meet in each other's and sometimes this is acceptable. There are, however, two distinct disadvantages in using a private house. One is that unless the room is very large indeed, it cannot expand sufficiently to increase membership when the opportunity arises. (All clubs benefit from new members coming in with fresh ideas.) Secondly, a private home tends to bear the personality of its owner and this can sometimes be to a society's detriment. Far better to meet on a no-man's land where everybody is free to say what they think without fear of offending a generous hostess.

Before this first meeting, it is wise to have made tentative enquiries in the district by calling in at the Town Hall to ask for information on rooms, halls and meeting places of any kind which are available for hire. Possibilities include schools (but remember that primary schools often have only tiny chairs), community or health centres, the library, scout huts, works canteens, church halls, Y.W.C.A. buildings and rooms over public houses. You should have read local newspapers to see where other functions are held and followed them up so that the prices and facilities of each one can be discussed at this first meeting.

I think it is very important to choose a meeting place where the atmosphere is bright and cheerful. In the course of my travels, speaking to clubs of all shapes and sizes up and down the country, I have been struck by the immediate impact, good or bad, which some halls make. It would be impossible to generalize, but the appropriate size of hall to fit the number of members seems to be a very important factor and hall caretakers will know how many people can be comfortably accommodated on the premises. It is difficult to gauge how many prospective members will turn up, but on the whole, a smaller place which is full of people tends to engender a feeling of goodwill and comradeship. But if, from early enquiries, it appears that membership may be large—

play safe and go for a big hall, even if at first members rattle around like peas in a barrel.

Don't be persuaded to hire a room too far away from the area in which most members live. Investigate the car parking facilities along with the kitchen arrangements, the cloakroom and the provision of heating and lighting. We all know what it's like to sit in a cold draughty hall, but when a few miserable 40 watt bulbs shed gloom as well, it is difficult for members to become enthusiastic about anything.

Another question which must be considered is, 'Is the hall in a moderately quiet position?' Once, when speaking to a club I had a terrible time making myself heard above the roar of traffic changing gear at a main road junction. Another time at a meeting I attended in a hotel lounge, the noise from the bar next door defied all attempts to concentrate upon the business in hand. On one occasion, a jet aircraft coming in to land at a nearby runway actually brought the speaker to a dead stop. Not being used to this sound, she thought the plane was going to plough straight through the building.

If a hall is poorly decorated, but is otherwise satisfactory, consider making improvements. The Women's Institute in our village raised money and bought material for new curtains which members made themselves and they helped to pay for the decoration of the hall as well.

The day and time for future meetings

It will not be possible to fix the day and time definitely until members have been consulted at the inaugural public meeting. But research is needed to find out about other regular meetings which take place in the vicinity. Try to avoid clashing with popular classes held at local Colleges of Further Education which may draw off potential members. If there are other societies functioning, check on the times they meet. It may be very difficult to steer clear of every activity going on in a thriving town, but at least give plenty of thought to the matter. Much of the success of membership depends upon the choice of day and time.

Whether the meetings are to be held in the morning, afternoon or evening, or at weekly, fortnightly or monthly intervals will depend upon the age group and wishes of the majority of the members. In the case of a women's society, if a small room is provided for a crèche where older women can look after the offspring of the young mothers, then a morning or afternoon meeting may be the answer. Other women much prefer to leave their children behind them in the evenings when husbands can baby-sit, in which case seven-thirty would be more suitable.

The time you begin and finish meetings must also fit in with members' commitments. Have some of them to fetch children home from school? If so, arrange to close the meeting in time for mothers to collect them in comfort. Will some members need to travel to meetings by bus? Check on the services and announce them, so that potential members who do not live within walking distance of the hall are encouraged to join if the times are convenient.

Publicity

Decide upon the all important date for your inaugural public meeting, allowing time for a good deal of publicity to be executed.

The friendly letter

One idea for getting the public to come along to a meeting is to duplicate a friendly letter. The use of a duplicating machine can often be obtained through personal contact. If this is not possible, ask local businessmen or enquire at schools if anybody would be willing to run copies off cheaply for you. A large number of letters can then be produced without much difficulty, worded in the following vein.

Dear Resident,

A few of us on the Pedley Wood Estate have got together and decided that, although we love our children, it would be most refreshing to have an hour to ourselves once a week when we could enjoy new interests and make new friends.

We plan to start a Women's Club, meeting at Southbridge Junior School on Tuesday evenings at 7.30. Our first meeting will be on 5th October and we've lots of ideas and want to share them with you. We will plan for just a few weeks to get things going and then you and your friends can contribute your suggestions to help make a really interesting programme together.

We've heard some people say that living on this estate is lonely. If so, this club should soon solve that problem. Do come on Tuesday, 5th October, at 7.30 and meet us!

With best wishes,

Yours sincerely,

Mary Linfield.

P.S. If you are unable to come on this occasion but would like further information, please ring Southbridge 4545.

If these letters can be delivered by hand, with a few friendly words of encouragement to the recipient to join, this will repay handsomely. However, time is not always available to carry this out, in which case they can be pushed through letter boxes. Sometimes newsagents will pop one into each newspaper delivered in the locality.

Posters

Maybe somebody present at this first meeting knows a printer personally. If so, he or she may be able to persuade him to produce a number of posters at a reduced rate. Alternatively, contact the newspaper office and other printing works in the area and choose the lowest estimate offered.

The cheapest and most eye-catching posters are printed in large, bold, black letters on a yellow background. A good size is 20 inches high and 15 inches wide, because this doesn't take up too much space in shop windows. Remember that you need to allow up to four weeks for delivery especially if your order is undertaken at a reduced rate. The printer can then execute the work at his own convenience.

If you feel this is an extravagant way to advertise your society at this early stage, ask if anybody personally knows an art teacher, draughtsman or anyone else engaged in work of an artistic nature. Alternatively, it is possible that someone would undertake to produce a number of posters by hand, or show members how to make professional looking posters themselves. Further helpful information can be gleaned from a little book called *Lettering*, price 12½p, obtainable from The National Federation of Women's Institutes (address page 124).

Choosing the exact wording is very important and the message must be simple, pared down to the bare essentials and possible to read in three seconds.

It could look something like this:

TUESDAY 5TH OCTOBER

an

INVITATION FOR YOU

to

MAKE NEW FRIENDS!
FIND NEW INTERESTS!

at

The Pedley Wood Women's Society
Southbridge Junior School, 7.30 p.m.

or alternatively:

BORED? — LONELY?
JOIN US

on

TUESDAY 5TH OCTOBER

at

The Pedley Wood Women's Society
Southbridge Junior School, 7.30 p.m.

When the posters are ready for distribution, ask the following places if they would be willing to display one:—

> Public Library
> Public houses
> Citizen's Advice Bureau
> Town Hall
> Employment Exchange

In the case of a women's society, also:—

> Welfare clinics
> Shops used by women such as
> hairdressers, launderettes, super-
> markets, etc.

Don't be put off if you are sometimes refused. It is surprising how often one gets the most co-operation from the least likely quarters.

Local Newspapers
Ring up the local paper and ask to speak to the editor or whoever deals with items of news of this kind. Talk about the proposed club, offer an invitation to the first meeting and suggest that a feature might be written about it. Follow up the conversation with a letter confirming date and meeting place and briefly re-state the aims and objects of the club

and conclude the letter by offering to supply further information if required. It is also worth putting an advertisement in the personal column of the newspaper for the three weeks preceding the first public meeting, as many people read this section.

The inaugural public meeting

The main decisions to be put to the inaugural public meeting have already been discussed and if the preliminary work has been carefully carried out, then a large number of interested people should have been attracted to come along. See that the hall is brightly lit and warm, the chairs placed in readiness and water heating for coffee or tea, with cups and saucers set out on a table. Appoint a cheerful hostess to offer a word of welcome and show people to their seats.

At the front of the meeting, behind a table bearing a bowl of flowers, a jug of water and glasses, the agenda and other relevant literature, sit the chairman, the secretary and treasurer. Possibly a special guest has been invited who has some standing in the locality or a particular interest in the society. Punctually at the appointed time, the chairman should open the meeting and welcome the audience officially. This is followed by a description of the society with its aims and objects and proposed activities, both social and educational, together with the suggested figure for the subscription.

The open discussion which follows is, of course, a most important part of the meeting. All those present should be encouraged to offer their opinions and suggestions for the sort of things they hope the club will offer. The officers can add these ideas to their own and discover how best to satisfy the needs of this new society. And don't forget to take a vote on the day and time most suitable to the majority (see page 109).

The proposed constitution can be read and it should be explained that the present caretaker committee has only been temporarily elected for a period of three or six months, until members get to know each other and can choose their own leaders and committee.

Election of officers

From suggestions put forward by those in the audience, it will eventually become apparent who would be likely to make good future officers and committee members. What sort of qualities are required and what are their duties? It is difficult to generalize, but a *Chairman* should have a friendly manner, the ability to make quick decisions and a knowledge of the way in which meetings are handled. It is the chairman's job to be at the meetings early, to check up on details, greet members, open and close the meetings, introduce the speakers and thank them afterwards or detail someone else to do so. The agenda for the committee meetings will be arranged with the secretary beforehand. The chairman should keep the meeting to the point, tie up practical details, draw in shy committee members, keep a finger on the pulse of the society, and keep order tactfully.

A *Secretary* will book and prepare the hall for the meetings and check that committee members are doing their allocated tasks, such as putting out the chairs, tables and flowers, seeing that somebody is responsible for refreshments, receiving the speaker and helping with equipment. The job includes arranging for speakers and keeping an accurate record of minutes of business and committee meetings as well as a list of members' names and addresses. In fact, this person takes on a great deal of responsibility for the smooth running of any society, but will naturally collaborate with the chairman in everything.

A *Treasurer* should be an honest person, with simple arithmetical ability and an orderly mind who should keep an accurate record of accounts, pay the speakers' fees, see that subscriptions are collected and make sure that the club meets its financial obligations, such as payment for hire of hall and other expenditure.

How will these officers be elected when the time comes? It is usual for members of the club to put forward names two weeks before the voting always obtaining the consent of the person whose name is suggested. Ballot papers with the list of nominations should be prepared, stating clearly the actual number to be elected. The members obtaining the highest number of votes are 'in'.

The format of the future meetings

This will vary with each club, but here is a guide which can be adapted to suit your society.

> Chairman's opening remarks.
>
> Secretary reads minutes of the last meeting and makes special announcements and gives out notices, emphasizing important items and dates clearly.
>
> Chairman introduces the speaker.
>
> Speaker gives talk.
>
> Chairman invites questions from audience.
>
> Chairman calls on member to give vote of thanks.
>
> Refreshments are served.
>
> Any other business.
>
> Social time which can be a friendly chat, a short quiz, a game of musical chairs, bingo or a round of drinks. It all depends upon the type of club and what its members want.
>
> Chairman closes meeting with a few words or *God Save the Queen*.

Registering a new society

All new societies should open a bank account and if appropriate become a 'registered charity'. Further information on this very important asset can be obtained from local County Councils.

The inaugural public meeting is held in order to state the broad aims and objects and an outline of how the club is to be run; to find out if the need is really there; to gauge the enthusiasm of the audience; to establish the basic framework; to collect names and addresses of those who wish to join and if possible their annual subscription or at least a deposit towards it, so that the organizers have something in the kitty to defray expenses.

This is how a new society is born. Obviously, in a book of this nature there cannot be detailed methods and procedure laid down for running all types of society. Different problems and requirements produce the necessity for other rules and regulations, but further help can be gained from the following books: *Club Management*, published for the National Association of Women's Clubs, obtainable from The National Council of Social Service, price 17p. (This Association is also willing to help and advise small unattached women's groups—address, Appendix); *The Right Way to Conduct Meetings, Conferences and Discussions* by H. M. Taylor (Elliot Rightway Books), price 20p and obtainable from them (address page 122).

One last word. If attendance has been poor, do not despair. It often takes quite a while for a new idea to take root and bear fruit. Each person who *does* turn up can be urged to bring friends next time and providing there is the promise of an interesting speaker and the hint of a lively programme of activities in the future—the first round is won.

Conclusion

In the course of writing this book and talking to organizers of all types of club, I have been struck by how remarkably happy most of these people are. They lead active lives, involved with people in their community and automatically it seems, they become outgoing and well adjusted members of society.

Recently I met a married school teacher who had started a women's association twenty-five years ago. 'It's changed my life,' she said. 'Because of it, everything has been worth while'. And speaking to some of the one hundred and fifty members of this still flourishing club, it was obvious to me that this well loved woman had changed *their* lives for the better too. 'She helped me so much when my baby was ill,' said one. 'Without this club,' said another, 'I would never have lived through the time when my husband left me.' Or, 'We've had such good times. I wouldn't miss our Christmas Social for a Buckingham Palace Garden Party.'

I know of a young widow, driven to such desperation by the empty, lonely evenings that she put an advertisement in the personal column of her local newspaper. It ran: 'Lonely young widow proposes to start a club for members of either sex who are similarly placed. Please phone ——.' The result? She was inundated with phone calls and now organizes a number of clubs which anybody can join providing they live on their own. This girl says, 'To think what I would have missed if I hadn't had the courage to place that advertisement.'

These stories could be repeated a hundred times. New

life, new hope, more happiness and interests for many, many people who have taken a chance and seen what membership of a club can offer.

Loneliness has been proved to be one of the greatest enemies of our time. It claims victims who are both young and old, rich and poor, women whose children have left home, men who are widowed, retired couples and even the newly-weds living in a strange town. It often leads sufferers to the doctor's surgery or the hospital bed. Surely joining a club is a simple way to overcome this problem? Is it so simple that people don't even think of it? If the Women's Institutes had flourished in Norway in Ibsen's time, could he have found such poignant tragedies to write about?

A good club should be rather like the whole world in miniature. It should contain a little of everything—a fragment of all the exciting things which go towards making life worth living. It can exist for endless reasons. To stimulate, to instruct and edify, to chase boredom, to achieve perfection in some art, to serve others, have fun, and above all to make friends. Its members may be short or tall, fat or thin, clever or homely. The place of meeting may be a hay loft, a bar parlour, a church hall or the luxuriously appointed lounge of a four star hotel, but all these things are relatively unimportant. It all boils down to one basic truth. We shall get out of a club, as indeed out of life, whatever we are prepared to put into it.

Appendix of useful names and addresses

(The information below is correct at time of going to press)

Barnum's Carnival Novelties Ltd.,
67 Hammersmith Road,
London W14

Merry and Bright Ltd.,
118 Redbrook Road,
Barnsley,
Yorks

> Sell crepe paper in quantity cheaply.

BBC Ticket Unit,
Box WIA 1AA,
Broadcasting House,
London W1

The Publicity Office,
Broadcasting House,
5 Queen Street,
Edinburgh 2

Senior Producer of Light Entertainment,
Broadcasting House,
31-33 Newport Road,
Cardiff

The Ticket Unit,
Broadcasting House,
Piccadilly,
Manchester 1

Other Broadcasting Centres in all parts
of the country.

> Arrange visits to watch sound radio or television performances.

British Travel Association,
Tourist Information Centre,
64 St. James's Street,
London SW1

Produces monthly guide *Coming Events in Britain*.

Central Office of Information,
Distribution Unit,
Reference Division,
Hercules Road,
London SE1

Offers papers, pamphlets and factsheets on home and overseas affairs.

John Dron Ltd.,
Mountview House,
London N6 5BR

Supplies goods in bulk at reduced prices.

Elliot Rightway Books,
Kingswood,
Surrey

Sells book *The Right Way to Conduct Meetings, Conferences and Discussions*, price 20p.

English Folk Dance and Song Society,
Cecil Sharpe House,
2 Regents Park Road,
London W1

Helps and advises the public on folk dancing.

Entertainment Agents' Association,
3 Golden Square,
Piccadilly,
London W1

Mr Billy Butler,
23 Ranelagh Road,
Manchester,
M27 IHG

Will put you in touch with appropriate agents who handle bands, cabaret acts, pop stars and other personalities.

Film Distributors

British Transport Films,
Melbury House,
Melbury Terrace,
London NW1

Carlton Cine Service,
340 Carlton Hill,
Nottingham

Central Film Library
Government Building,
Bromyard Avenue,
Acton,
London W3

Central Film Library of Wales,
42 Cardiff Place,
Cardiff

Concord Film Council,
Nacton,
Ipswich,
Suffolk

Electricity Council Marketing Dept.,
Film Library,
Trafalgar Building,
1 Charing Cross,
London SW1

Supply catalogues or lists covering a wide range of subjects.

Gas Film Library,
6-7 Great Chapel Street,
London W1

Golden Film Library,
Stewart House,
Frances Road,
Windsor,
Bucks

Imperial Chemical Industry,
Film Library,
Thames House North,
Millbank,
London SW1

Intercontinental Films,
90 Merthyr,
Mawr Road,
Bridgend,
Glamorgan

Midland Film Library,   Supply catalogues or lists
137 Vicarage Road,   covering a wide range of
Langley,   subjects.
Oldbury,
Nr. Birmingham

Petroleum Films Bureau,
4 Brook Street,
Hanover Square,
London W1

Ranelagh Cine Services, Ltd.,
135 Prescott Road,
Liverpool 7

Scottish Central Film Library,
16/17 Woodside Terrace,
Charing Cross,
Glasgow C3

Sound Services Ltd.,
Kingston Road,
Merton Park,
London SW19

Homburgs Theatrical Agency,   Offers a wide selection of
31 Call Lane,   theatrical costumes.
Leeds 1

Mobile Discotheque Sounds Systems,
22 Baker Street,
London W1

Provides discotheques; disc jockeys; special lighting; disco girls. Countrywide service.

National Association of Women's Clubs,
26 Bedford Square,
London WC1 B 3HU

Sells book *Club Management*, price 17p.

National Federation of Women's Institutes,
39 Eccleston Square,
Victoria,
London SW1

Sells book *Lettering*, price 12½p

Performing Right Society,
29-33 Berners Street,
London W1

Provides information regarding copyright of sheet music, songs, etc.

Phonographic Performance, Ltd,
62 Oxford Street,
London W1

Provides information regarding copyright and use of gramophone records at public functions.

Keith Prowse Music Publishing
Company Ltd.,
21 Denmark Street,
London W1

Publishes old time songs, ballads and sketches.

Thames Launches, Ltd,
York Villa,
Church Street,
Twickenham,
Middlesex

Offers launches for private hire for outings.

Tufty Club National Organiser,
Royal Society for the Prevention of Accidents,
Terminal House,
52 Grosvenor Gardens,
London SW1

Issues information on the Tufty Clubs.

Index